A MAN OF
MY WORDS

A MAN OF MY WORDS

Reflections on the English Language

Richard Lederer

ST. MARTIN'S PRESS   NEW YORK

www.stmartins.com

ISBN 0-312-31785-9

10 9 8 7 6 5 4 3

To my partners on *A Way with Words*—
Charles Harrington Elster,
Stefanie Levine,
and Jill Fritz

CONTENTS

~⌒

CONTENTS

CONTENTS

ACKNOWLEDGMENTS

Thanks to Rabbi Robert Schenkerman for his contributions to "Oys and Joys"; to my *A Way with Words* cohost, Charles Harrington Elster, for his hand in shaping "A Declaration of Linguistic Independence" and "A Noo-kyuh-lur Nonproliferation Treatise"; to Barbara Berti for permission to use the excerpts from my appearance on *The Jim Bohannon Show*; to Gloria Rosenthal, not only for creating and running the Wonderful World of Words weekend, but for helping so much with the writing of "A Wordy Weekend"; and to my verbivorous editor Marian Lizzi for her loving labors on behalf of this book. Versions of "Stamp Out Fadspeak!" and "How Wise Is Proverbial Wisdom?" first appeared in *Verbatim* and "A Declaration of Linguistic Independence" in my foreword to *Dictionary of Americanisms* (John Wiley & Sons, 2003).

INTRODUCTION:

CONFESSIONS

OF A VERBIVORE

One day I found myself chatting with Mrs. Marilyn Frazier's class of sixth-grade students at Broken Ground School in Concord, New Hampshire, about the joys of language and the challenges of the writing life. During the question-and-answer session that followed, one of the boys in the class asked me, "Mr. Lederer, where do you get your ideas for your books?"

Ever since I became a writer, I had found that question to be the most difficult to answer and had only recently come up with an analogy that I thought would satisfy both my audience and me. Pouncing on the opportunity to unveil my spanking new explanation for the first time, I countered with "Where does the spider get its web?"

The idea, of course, was that the spider is not aware of how it spins out intricate and beautiful patterns with the silky material that is simply a natural part of itself. Asking a writer to account for the genesis of his or her ideas is as futile as asking a spider to explain the source of its web and the method of its construction.

So when the young man asked his question, I replied, "Where does the spider get its web?"

He shot right back, "From its butt!"

Since that visit, I've checked out the boy's assertion, and, sure enough, spiders do produce their silk in glands located in their posteriors. The glands open through the tiny spinnerets located at the hind end of the abdomen. Well, it may be that for lo these many years I've been talking and writing through my butt, but that doesn't stop me from being a self-confessed and unrepentant verbivore.

Carnivores eat flesh and meat; piscivores eat fish; herbivores consume plants and vegetables; verbivores devour words. I am such a creature. My whole life I have feasted on words— ogled their appetizing shapes, colors, and textures; swished them around in my mouth; lingered over their many tastes; let their juices run down my chin. During my adventures as a fly-by-the-roof-of-the-mouth, user-friendly wizard of idiom, I have met thousands of other wordaholics, logolepts, and verbivores, folks who also eat their words.

What is there about words that makes a language person love them so? The answers are probably as varied as the number of verbivores themselves. There are as many reasons to love words as there are people who love them. How do we love thee, language? Let me count the ways.

Some word people are intrigued by the birth and life of words. They become enthusiastic, ebullient, and enchanted when they discover that *enthusiastic* literally means "possessed by a god," *ebullient* "boiling over, spouting out," and *enchanted* "singing a magic song." They are rendered starry-eyed by the insight that *disaster* (*dis-aster*) literally means "ill-starred" and intoxicated by the information that *intoxicated* has poison in its heart. They love the fact that *amateur* is cobbled from the very first verb that all students of Latin learn—*amo:* "I love."

Wordsters of etymological persuasion also love to track down the origins of phrases. Take the particularly elusive quarry *the whole nine yards*. The fact that no printed citation exists for *the whole nine yards* prior to 1967 renders dubious the nautical theory that the expression refers to the nine sails on a three square-masted rigger. Nor could *the whole nine yards*, which means "the whole shootin' match," "whole hog," "the whole ball of wax," issue from football, in which a team must gain ten, not nine, yards to reach a first down. Equally un-proven or provably wrong are dozens of other etymological explanations, including the material to make a dress, bridal veil, or Scottish kilt; the length of a machine-gun belt in World War II fighter planes; the height of a prison retaining wall; and the volume of mined ore.

My research indicates that *the whole nine yards* refers to the revolving barrels on the backs of concrete mixing trucks. These barrels held a volume of nine cubic yards (they're now twelve cubic yards) in the early 1960s, a fact that explains why I never heard the phrase when I was growing up in the 1950s. Emptying the entire contents was one humongous road job—and, in most states, illegal because the weight of such a load would exceed the per-axle limits.

As you can see, my explanations are never in the ab-stract—and always in the concrete.

Still another denomination of verbivore sees words as col-lections of letters to be juggled, shuffled, and flipped. Inspired by the word *bookkeeper,* with its three consecutive pairs of double letters, these logologists fantasize about a biologist who helps maintain raccoon habitats: *a raccoon nook keeper*—six consecutive sets of double letters—and another biologist who studies the liquid secreted by chickadee eggs. They call this scientist a *chickadee egg goo-ologist*—and into the world are born three consecutive pairs of triple letters!

Then there's the breed of logophile who enjoys trying to turn the brier patch of pronoun cases, subject-verb agreement, sequence of tenses, and the indicative and subjunctive moods into a manageable garden of delight. Such devotees of correct usage often explore the nuances of confusing word pairs—*take* versus *bring* (you take out the garbage; you bring in the newspaper), *podium* versus *lectern* (you stand on a podium; you stand behind a lectern), and *comprise* versus *compose* (they're antonyms, not synonyms: the large comprises the small; the small composes the large).

Throughout my adventures of a verbivore, I have striven mightily to teach the difference between the verbs *lie* and *lay*. *Lie* means "to repose"; *lay* means "to put." *Lie* is intransitive; it never takes an object. *Lay* is transitive; it always takes an object. Pardon the fowl language, but a hen on its back is lying. A hen on its stomach may be laying—an egg.

Alas, all my efforts have been swept away by the Enron debacle. Here's a little ditty I've written about the company that made an end run around ethics. Please recall that the disgraced CEO of the company was Kenneth Lay:

Take the Money Enron

The difference between "lie" and "lay"
Has fallen into deep decay.
But now we know from Enron's shame
That Lay and "lie" are just the same.

Among my favorite wordmongers are those who prowl the lunatic fringes of language, *lunatic* because the ancients believed that prolonged exposure to the moon (Latin *luna*) rendered one moonstruck, or daft. These recreational wordplayers wonder why we drive in a parkway and park in a driveway, why our nose can run and our feet can smell, why the third hand on a clock is called the second hand, and why, if adults commit adultery, infants don't commit infantry. Why is it, they muse, that a man puts on a pair of pants but a woman puts on only one bra? Why is it that a man can call a woman a vision, but not a sight—unless his eyes are sore?

Finally, there are the legions of pundits, punheads, and pun pals who tell of the Buddhist who said to the hot dog vendor, "Make me one with everything." That's the same Buddhist who never took Novocain when he had teeth extracted because he wished to transcend dental medication. These punderful verbivores become even bigger hot dogs when they tell about Charlemagne, who mustered his Franks and set out with great relish to assault and pepper the Saracens, but he couldn't catch up. (Frankly, I never sausage a pun. It's the wurst!)

At rare times, all these elements come together in a single word. Has there ever been another word as human as *usher*? In sound and meaning it is not a paragon among words, but it accommodates the full spectrum of humankind. Words and people have always hung around together, and within the brief compass of the five letters in *usher* we find the pronouns *us*, *she*, *he*, and *her*. Like humanity, *usher* has a long history, going all the way back to the Latin *ostium*, "door," related to *os*, "mouth," because a door was likened to the mouth of a building. So there again is that iron link between things and human beings.

Usher winkingly reminds us that all words are created by

people, and that language unfailingly reflects the fearful asymmetry of our kind. Thus, even though writers write, bakers bake, hunters hunt, preachers preach, and teachers teach, grocers don't groce, butchers don't butch, carpenters don't carpent, milliners don't millin, haberdashers don't haberdash—and ushers don't ush.

I am heels over head in love with language. When I say *heels over head*, rather than *head over heels*, I am not two letters short of a complete alphabet or a syllable short of a coherent statement. *Head over heels* is the normal position, sort of like doing things ass backwards, which is the way we do everything. I don't know about you, but when I flip over something, my heels are over my head.

When I say *language*, I mean by and large that glorious, uproarious, outrageous, courageous, stupendous, tremendous, end-over-endous adventure we call the English language. That's because in matters verbal I am unabashedly lexist. Just as many would say that, among many other things, the Italians do food well and that, among their many other accomplishments, the French do style and fashion well, I believe that we English speakers and writers do language especially well. One might say that we do it lexicellently. This book chronicles my heels-over-head love affair with English. May you have a wordaholic, logoleptic, and verbivorous time sharing that joyride with me.

Richard Lederer
San Diego, California
richard.lederer@pobox.com

A

CELEBRATION

OF

ENGLISH

OUR ABOUNDING

ENGLISH LANGUAGE

The other day I went to the bookstore to buy a dictionary. The clerk showed me a really cheap one. I couldn't find the words to thank her.

Then she directed me to a thesaurus. I thought that was an accommodating, altruistic, benevolent, caring, compassionate, considerate, courteous, decent, empathic, gracious, kind, magnanimous, nice, obliging, solicitous, sweet, and thoughtful thing to do.

The multitudinous choice of words in English offers both a delightful and daunting challenge to native and nonnative speakers. In William Styron's *Sophie's Choice*, the heroine, Polish-born Sophie, expresses mock horror at the infinite variety of English words:

"Such a language! . . . Too many words. I mean just the word for *vélocité*. I mean *fast*. *Rapid*. *Quick*. All the same thing! A scandal!"

"*Swift?*" I added.

"How about *speedy?*" Nathan asked.

9

"*Hasty?*" I went on.

"And *fleet?*" Nathan said. "Though that's a bit fancy."

"Stop it!" Sophie said, laughing. "Too much! Too many words, this English. In French it is so simple. You just say *vite*."

You should not be aghast, alarmed, amazed, appalled, astonished, bewildered, blown away, bowled over, confounded, dumbfounded, electrified, flabbergasted, flummoxed, overwhelmed, shocked, startled, stunned, stupefied, surprised, taken aback, or thunderstruck at this capacious cornucopia of synonyms in our marvelous language.

English boasts by far the largest number of words of all languages, 616,500 officially enshrined in the *Oxford English Dictionary*. That's almost four times the vocabulary size of its nearest competitor, German; five times the size of Russian, in third place; and six times the size of Spanish and French, tied for fourth. As a result, English possesses a plethora of synonyms that allow greater nuances of meaning than are available in other tongues.

A recent *New Yorker* cartoon puckishly celebrated our linguistic treasure trove. The cartoon's caption read: "Roget's Brontosaurus," and pictured was a big dinosaur in whose thought bubble appeared: "Large, great, huge, considerable, bulky, voluminous, ample, massive, capacious, spacious, mighty, towering, monstrous . . ." If not for the finite capacity of thought bubbles, the artist could have added: "big, Brobdingnagian, colossal, enormous, gargantuan, gigantic, grand, hefty, hulking, humongous, husky, immense, jumbo, leviathan, looming, lumbering, mammoth, mountainous, ponderous, prodigious, sizable, substantial, tremendous, vast, weighty, whopping."

Such a cartoon would be far less likely to appear in a magazine printed in a language other than English. Books like

Roget's Thesaurus are foreign to speakers of most other languages. Given the scope of their vocabularies, they have little need of them.

I hesitate to conclude this song of praise to the glories of English with dark news. But I regret to inform you that yesterday, a senior editor of *Roget's Thesaurus* assumed room temperature, bit the dust, bought the farm, breathed his last, came to the end of the road, cashed in his chips, cooled off, croaked, deep-sixed, expired, gave up the ghost, headed for the hearse, headed for the last roundup, kicked off, kicked the bucket, lay down one last time, lay with the lilies, left this mortal plain, met his maker, met Mr. Jordan, passed away, passed in his checks, passed on, perished, permanently changed his address, pulled the plug, pushed up daisies, returned to dust, slipped his cable, slipped his mortal coil, sprouted wings, took the dirt nap, took the last long count, traveled to kingdom come, turned up his toes, went across the creek, went belly up, went to glory, went the way of all flesh, went to his final reward, went west—and, of course, he died.

DOING A NUMBER ON ENGLISH

Recently, some organizations in Germany joined forces to compile a list of the hundred words that best reflect the twentieth century. *AIDS, beat, bikini, camping, comics, computer, design, Holocaust, image, jeans, pop, sex, single, star, stress*—English words that became part of the German language during the past hundred years—are featured in the list. That's just one piece of evidence that English has become the closest thing that humankind has ever had to a universal language.

"I think that language is a mirror of history, and these words reflect that," said Karin Frank-Cyrus, head of the Society for German Language. "The English language has become a lingua franca, a language that the whole world understands."

It is said again and again these days that there are lies, damnable lies, and statistics. Nonetheless, Americans are fascinated with and by statistics and take a special interest in facts that can be quantified. Here are some essential facts about our English tongue, expressed statistically:

Number of languages in the world: Approximately 6,800, 50 to 90 percent of which will be extinct in a hundred years.

Number of people around the world who can be reached by English in some form: 1,500,000,000.

Percentage of those people who learned English as a second (or third or fourth) language: 51.5. China and India each have more speakers of English than the United States.

Number of countries or territories in which English has official status: 87.

Percentage of the world's English speakers who live in the largest English-speaking country, the United States: 20.

Percentage of world English that is American English: 66.

Percentage of world English that is British English: 16.

Percentage of students in the European Union studying English: 83.

Percentage of people in the European Union who are fluent in English: 75.

Percentage of nonnative speakers around the world who are fluent in English: 25.

Doing a Number on English

Percentage of all books in the world printed in English: *50*.

Percentage of international telephone calls made in English: *52*.

Percentage of radio programs worldwide broadcast in English: *60*.

Percentage of global box office from films in English: *63*.

Percentage of global E-mail in English: *68*.

Percentage of international mail and telexes written and addressed in English: *70*.

Percentage of global computer text stored in English: *80*.

Percentage of the 12,500 international organizations in the world that make use of the English language: *85*.

Percentage of those international organizations that use English exclusively: *33*.

Percentage of all English words throughout history that no longer exist: *85*.

Number of words listed in the *Oxford English Dictionary*, not counting its supplements: *616,500*.

Average number of words added to English each year: *1,000*.

Number of words in the largest dictionaries of German, the world's second largest language: *185,000*.

Number of words in the largest dictionaries of Russian, the world's third largest language: *130,000*.

Number of words in the largest dictionaries for French and Spanish, tied for the world's fourth largest language: *100,000*.

Borrowed words in English vs. native (Anglo-Saxon) words, expressed as a ratio: *3:1*.

Number of languages in the English vocabulary: *300*.

Percentage of English words made from Latin word parts: *50*.

Number of words the average English speaker actually recognizes: *10,000–20,000*.

Percentage of the average English speaker's conversation made up of the most frequently used 737 words: *96*.

OYS AND JOYS

For centuries, fair-haired sea rovers from North Germany—Angles, Saxons, and Jutes—habitually cruised about the British coast in beaked Viking ships and attacked cities for booty and a lust for battle. In the middle of the fifth century, around A.D. 449, these Anglo-Saxon plunderers sailed across the North Sea and came to the islands then known as Britannia. They found the countryside pleasant and the people fighting among each other easy to conquer, and so they remained there and took the land for themselves. That is how Anglo-Saxons came to be the ancestors of the English and why English is, at its heart, a Germanic language. The hundred most frequently used words in English are all of Anglo-Saxon origin, as are eighty-three of the next hundred.

Two women of exceeding importance to my life have helped to bring home to me the continuing influence of the Germanic tongues on our English language.

My mother, Leah Perowoski Lederer, was born in the United States at the very end of the nineteenth century, after her father, mother, and older brothers and sister had come over here from Vilna, Russia (now Lithuania). Mother's first language was Yiddish, but, like all the other parents in our West Philadelphia neighborhood, she spoke Yiddish as a way of keeping us children from understanding what was being said. If immigrants were going to become Americans, they must speak English—and English only! But in the process of Americanizing, many of us second-generation American Jews lost part of our heritage. We lost a language handed down from generation to generation and from nation to nation, full of humor and self-deprecating wit and sarcasm and enriched with raw idioms, target-accurate expressions, and sayings that exude a magic and laughter, blended with sober reality.

When Isaac Bashevis Singer was awarded the Nobel Prize for Literature in 1978, he remarked in his acceptance speech: "The high honor bestowed upon me is also a recognition of the Yiddish language—a language of exile, without a land, without frontiers, not supported by any government, a language which possesses no words for weapons, ammunition, military exercises, war tactics. There is a quiet humor in Yiddish and a gratitude for every day of life, every crumb of success, each encounter of love. In a figurative way, Yiddish is the wise and humble language of us all, the idiom of a frightened and hopeful humanity."

The word *Yiddish* derives from the German *judisch*, "Jewish." The principal parent of Yiddish is High German, the form of German encountered by Jewish settlers from northern France in the eleventh century. Yiddish, a language written in the characters of the Hebrew alphabet and from right to left, has enjoyed borrowing words from Russian, Polish, English, and all the other languages and countries along the routes that

Jews have traveled during the past thousand years. Journalist Charles Rappaport once quipped, "I speak ten languages—all of them Yiddish."

Although Yiddish has been in danger of dying out for a thousand years, the language is spoken today by millions of people throughout the world—in Russia, Poland, Romania, France, England, Israel, Africa, Latin America, New Zealand, Australia, Canada, and the United States, where, like the bagel, it was leavened on both coasts, in New York and Hollywood. It is spoken even in Transylvania: A beautiful girl awakens in bed to find a vampire at her side. Quickly she holds up a cross. "Zie gernisht helfen," laughs the vampire. Translation: "It won't do you any good."

Most of us already speak a fair amount of Yiddish without fully realizing that we do. Almost a hundred Yiddish words have become part of our everyday conversations, including:

cockamamy: mixed-up, ridiculous.

fin: slang for five-dollar bill, from *finf,* the Yiddish word for "five."

glitch: an error or malfunction in a plan or machine.

gun moll: a double clipping of *gonif's Molly,* Yiddish for "thief's woman."

kibitzer: one who comments, often in the form of unwanted advice, during a game, often cards.

maven: expert.

mazuma: money.

mish-mosh: a reduplication for a mess.

schlep: to drag or haul.

schlock: shoddy, cheaply produced merchandise.

schmeer: the entire deal, the whole package.

schmooze: to converse informally.

schnoz: nose.

yenta: a blabbermouth, gossip, woman of low origins.

. . . and so on through the whole *megillah,* or long, involved story.

A number of poignant Yiddish words defy easy translation into English:

chutzpah: nerve, unmitigated gall, a quality we admire within ourselves, but never in others. The classic definition of *chutzpah* is the quality demonstrated by the man who killed his mother and father and then threw himself on the mercy of the court because he was an orphan.

kvell: to show enormous pride in the accomplishments of one's children.

mensch: a real authentic human being—a person.

naches: the glow of pleasure-plus-pride that only a child can give to its parents: "This is my son, the *doctor!*"

oy; oy vay; oy vay is mir: literally, "Oh, pain," but not so much words as an entire vocabulary. Oy *vay* and *oy* can express any emotion from mild pleasure to vaulting pride, from mild relief to lament through a vale of tears. Albert Einstein's theory of relativity laid the theoretical foundation for the building of the atom bomb. When the great scientist received the news of the mass destruction wrought by the bombs dropped on Hiroshima and Nagasaki, he reacted with two Yiddish words often invoked in such black circumstances: "Oy vay."

tsuris: the gamut of painful emotions—some real, some imagined, some self-inflicted.

Yiddish is especially versatile in describing those poor souls who inhabit the world of the ineffectual, and each is assigned a distinct place in the gallery of pathetic types: *schmo, schmendrick, schnook, schmegegge, schlep, schlub, schmuck, putz, klutz, kvetch,* and *nudnick.* Yiddish readily coins new names for new, pitiable personalities: a *nudnick* is a pest; a *phudnick* is a nudnick with a Ph.D. The rich nuances that suffuse this roll call are seen in the timeless distinction between a *schlimeil,* "a clumsy jerk," and a *schlimazel,* "a habitual loser": the schlimeil inevitably trips and spills his hot soup—all over the schlimazel. (And the nebbish is the one who has to clean it up.)

Yiddish never apologizes for what it is—the earthy, wise soul of an expressive people who have learned that life is but a mingled yarn, good and ill together. Which reminds me of the *zaftig* ("buxom, well-rounded") blonde who wears an enormous ring to a charity ball. "It happens to be the third most famous diamond in the whole world," she boasts. "The first is the Hope diamond, then comes the Kohinoor, and then comes this one, which is called the Lipschitz."

"What a stone! How lucky you are!"

"Wait, wait," says the lady. "Nothing in life is all *mazel* ['good luck']. Unfortunately, with this famous Lipschitz diamond comes also the famous Lipschitz curse."

Gasping, the other women ask, "And what is this famous Lipschitz curse?"

"Lipschitz," sighs the lady.

Then there is the even less famous *Lederer* curse, borne by my wife, Simone. Near the end of 1991, I committed an act of public matrimony. My coconspirator was Simone van Egeren, whose last name reveals that she is of Dutch descent. She was born in Rotterdam and came to the United States at the age of four. Throughout my relationship with my Dutch treat, I've been enjoying saucy Holland days.

Actually, I'm somewhat embarrassed to be such a lover of the English language and married to a Dutch woman. For one thing, we English speakers have used the word *Dutch* in confusing and derogatory ways. Probably no other nationality but Dutch has come in for so consistent a torrent of verbal abuse from the British, their neighbors across the North Sea. In dozens of compound words and expressions, the Dutch are depicted as cowardly, cheap, or deceitful.

Take the word *Yankee*, which has had its ups and downs during its several-hundred-year history. The Dutch love for cheese was well known, and *Yankee* was first an ethnic insult that British colonists hurled at Dutch freebooters in early New York. The British fashioned *Yankee* from the Dutch *Jan Kaas*, which literally meant "John Cheese," combining the common Dutch first name *Jan* (pronounced "Yahn") with *Kaas* (the

Dutch word for "cheese," the country's national product). Over time, the ethnic slur got blurred into *Yankee*. After a while, the feisty American revolutionaries were given the name by the loyal British. The song "Yankee Doodle" was originally one of derision, sung by British soldiers to mock the poorly clothed colonists. But the colonial army gave the melody new lyrics and adopted it as a robust and proud marching song.

While Simone and I were courting, we invited friends to go out with us for dinner and they insisted on going "Dutch treat." Simone knew that the phrase was negative—a Dutch treat (or going Dutch) isn't a treat at all because each guest pays his or her own way—but she wondered why. In my search for an answer, I discovered more than sixty disparaging Dutch compounds and expressions in the English language, including:

double Dutch: Gibberish; the kind of talk deliberately intended to confuse the listener.

Dutch act (also *to do the Dutch*): Suicide.

Dutch auction: One that reverses the order of an ordinary auction; it starts with high figures and regresses to lower ones.

Dutch bargain: A one-sided deal, not a bargain at all.

Dutch comfort: Small comfort, if any; typified by the line, "Well, it could have been worse."

Dutch courage: The kind of bravery that comes out of a bottle. As far back as 1625, the British poet Edmund Waller wrote:

"The Dutch their wine and all their brandy lose, / Disarmed of that from which their courage grows."

Dutch defense: Retreat or surrender.

Dutch leave: To be AWOL.

Dutch reckoning: Guesswork; a disputed bill.

Dutch uncle: Not an uncle at all, but an old busybody who reprimands or lectures a young person.

Why have the good people of the Netherlands been made to suffer so in English parlance? Why are the Dutch so *in Dutch* (meaning "in trouble") in our idioms? Until well after Shakespeare's time, the Dutch were highly regarded in most literary references by British authors. But during the seventeenth century, the two nations became rivals in international commerce, fighting for control of the sea and parts of the New World. For a number of years the Dutch colonial empire loomed as the chief threat to the British, so the disrespectful references began. Even when the British and Dutch empires ceased their conflicts, the slurs on the Dutch crossed the ocean from the British Isles to the United States.

Growing up speaking a lot of Dutch at home, Simone felt ambivalently about her native tongue. Although she loved the sound of Dutch, she believed it to be an unglamorous language. "People around the world speak English, Spanish, and French, but almost nobody speaks Dutch but the Dutch," she said.

Simone's heart was warmed when I showed her that Dutch teems our English tongue. Our *cop*, for example, comes from a Dutch word that means "to seize or catch." *Dote* derives from a Dutch word that signifies "to be silly," the meaning of which we see more clearly in our words *dotage* and *dotty*. *Easel* is built from Dutch word material that means "little ass," because the artist's stand acts as a small beast of burden. *Filibuster*, borrowed from the Dutch *vrijbuiter*, "freebooter," first meant "pirate, adventurer" in English, a sense retained in the current denotation of *filibuster*: "holding a piece of legislation captive by making long and windy speeches."

Quack, in the sense of bogus doctor, descends from the Dutch compound *quacksalver*, which itself is cobbled from *quack*, "to make a sound like a duck," *salve*, "ointment," and *-er*, "one who." In days of yore, a quacksalver was a snake oil doctor who traveled about hawking (quacking) all the maladies his unguent, or salve, could cure.

When the Dutch came to the New World, the figure of Saint Nikolaas, their patron saint, was on the first ship. The pronunciation of *Saint Nikolaas* became folk etymologized, and the English in New York heard their Dutch neighbors saying *Sinterklaas*. They recognized the Dutch name Klaas and thought they were hearing "Santa Klaas." After the Dutch lost control of New Amsterdam to the English in the seventeenth century, *Sinterklaas* gradually became anglicized into *Santa Claus* and acquired some of the features of the British Father Christmas.

It is time to cut through the poppycock (from the Dutch *pappekak*, "soft dung") by noting the enormous contributions that the Dutch language has made to British and American English. A partial list of gifts from our Netherfriends embraces *barracks, bedspread, boodle, boor, booze, boss, boy, brandy, bully, bulwark, bumpkin, buoy, bush, caboose, coleslaw, cookie, cruise, cruller, cuspidor, date, deck, decoy, dingus, dope, dumb, excise, furlough, gas, gin, golf, groove, halibut, hay, hobble, hop* (plant), *hose* (stockings), *huckster, husk, hustle, jib, kit, knapsack, landscape, loiter, luck, mangle, mart, pickle, pit* (in fruit), *placard, rack, school* (of fish), *scow, skate, sketch, sled, sleigh, sloop, slur, smuggle, snap, snatch, snoop, snort, snow, snuff, splint, spook, spool, stoker, stoop* (porch), *tackle* (fishing), *uproar, waffle, wagon, walrus, wiseacre,* and *yawl.*

The Dutch themselves have not retaliated in kind, and their language is free of mean-spirited English treats, English uncles, and English courage. Those who fail to recognize our linguistic debt to the Dutch will soon find themselves in deep trouble—in English.

A GUIDE TO BRITSPEAK, A TO ZED

The summer after we were married, Simone and I spent ten smashingly lovely honeymoon days on vacation (what the Brits call holiday) exploring the southwest of Britain. We took a drive and walk through time from the ancient stone mysteries at Stonehenge and Avebury to the modern glitz of Manchester's Granada Studios—Great Britain's answer to our Universal Studios theme park.

Confident that the island natives spoke our language, we expected few communication problems. We did, however, encounter a number of strange words and locutions that you should know when you visit the U.K. (United Kingdom). To clear the fog and unravel some transatlantic tangles, I offer here a selective list of differences between our English and British English. After all, I don't want you to miss the delights of Great Britain just because of a little thing like a language barrier.

If you choose to rent an automobile in the U.K., with it will come a whole new vocabulary. Be sure to fill it with petrol, not gas. Remember that the trunk is the boot, the hood is the bonnet (what the Brits call a hood is our convertible top), tires are tyres (and they have tracks, not treads), a headlight is a headlamp, the transmission is the gearbox, the windshield is the windscreen, a fender is a wing, and the muffler is a silencer.

Station wagons (waggons in Britspell) that speed by you are called estate cars or hatchbacks, trucks are lorries, and streetcars trams. Most British drivers (motorists) belong to AA—the Automobile Association, of course!

Our buses are their coaches. When a hotel in the British Isles posts a sign proclaiming, NO FOOTBALL COACHES ALLOWED, the message is not directed at the Vince Lombardis and Joe Paternos of the world. "No football coaches allowed" means "No soccer buses permitted."

While you are driving down the motorway (highway) and busily converting kilometres into miles, you must note that, in matters automotive, the Queen's English can be as far apart as the lanes on a dual carriageway (divided highway). A traffic circle is a roundabout, an intersection a junction, an overpass a flyover, a circular road around a city a ringway or orbital, a place to pull off the road a lay-by, a road shoulder a verge, and a railroad (railway) crossing a level crossing. All the time, you must be sure to stay to the left, not the right! As the joke goes, why did the Siamese twins go to England? Answer: So that the other one could drive.

When you have to use the subway in London, you should follow signs to the underground (informally, the tube). When you get on and off the underground, you'll hear a polite voice on the loudspeaker warning you to "mind the gap." That message means, "Look out for the space between the train and the platform." As you make your way upward to the streets of London, be aware that "Way out" is not a vestigial hippie expression. "Way out" signifies an exit.

If you decide to walk somewhere, you'll have to bear in mind that what a North American calls a sidewalk is an English pavement, while an American pavement is an English roadway. If someone directs you to the Circus, don't head for a big top. Rather, look for a large circle (Piccadilly Circus is rather like Columbus Circle in New York) where several streets converge.

At the end of World War II, Winston Churchill tells us, the Allied leaders nearly came to blows over a single word during their negotiations when some diplomats suggested that it was time to "table" an important motion. For the British, *table* meant that the motion should be put on the table for discussion. For the Americans it meant just the opposite—that it should be put on the shelf and dismissed from discussion.

Also at the end of the war, the British government made an urgent request for thousands of bushels of corn. So the U.S. government shipped just what the Brits asked for—corn. What the British officials really wanted was wheat. Had they wanted corn, they would have called it "maize" or specified "Indian corn."

Many of the most beguiling misunderstandings can arise where identical words have different meanings in the two cultures and lingoes. When an American exclaims, "I'm mad about my flat," she is upset about her punctured tire. When a Brit exclaims, "I'm mad about my flat," she is exulting about her apartment. When a Brit rails against "that bloody villain," he is describing the dastard's immoral character, not his physical condition. When a Brit points out that you have "a ladder in your hose," the situation is not as bizarre as you might at first think. Quite simply, you have a run in your stocking.

Some of this bilingual confusion can get downright embarrassing: When Brits tell you that they will "come by in the morning and knock you up," they are informing you that they will wake you up with a knock on your door. (Similarly, a "knock up" in tennis means, simply, to hit the ball around.)

When a Brit offers to show you his collection of bloomers, he means his examples of bloopers, or verbal faux pas. When a Londoner wants to take you "to the BM," she is talking about the British Museum. When a Brit volunteers to take you to a solicitor, that's a trip to a general-practice lawyer. When a Brit asks you if you need a rubber, she is trying to make your writing safer. English rubbers are erasers. When a Brit tells you how marvelously "homely" you are, that's a compliment. He means that you are domestic and home loving. In the U.K. it is quite possible to be both homely and attractive at the same time.

In the early part of this century, Finley Peter Dunne's Mr. Dooley wryly observed, "When the American people get through with the English language, it will look as if it has been run over by a musical comedy." And as recently as 1974, Morton Cooper sneered meanly that "giving the English language to the Americans is like giving sex to small children; they know it's important, but they don't know what to do with it." A message on a London theater (theatre) marquee went so far as to advertise, AMERICAN WESTERN FILM — ENGLISH SUBTITLES. A London store sign announced, ENGLISH SPOKEN HERE — AMERICAN UNDERSTOOD.

With the increasing influence of film, radio, television, and international travel, the two mainstreams of the English language are rapidly converging like the streets of a circus. Still, there are scores of words, phrases, spellings, and constructions about which Brits and Yanks just don't agree. During a transatlantic telephone conversation, one of my British publishers told me that my book was attracting considerable newspaper coverage and she would be sure to send me the "cuttings." I asked her what she called the sections of plants one gets from gardens. She answered, "Those are clippings, of course." Of course—and not surprising in a land where the beer and Coke are warm and the toast is cold.

Here's a pop quiz that will help you discover how "bilingual" you are. Answers repose on page 283.

1. Look over these words and compound words that occur in both Britspeak and American. Then ask yourself what each one means in British English: *billion, biscuit, bitter, bob, braces, catapult, chemist, chips, crisps, dinner jacket, full stop, ground floor, hockey, ice, jelly, knickers, lift, M.P., minister, plaster, pocketbook, public school, pudding, spectacles, stone, stuff, sweet, till, tin, torch, vest, waistcoat.*

2. What would the average Brit call each of these words and compounds? *aisle, bar, bathroom, bobby pin, clothespin, counterclockwise, hardware store, intermission, kerosene, napkin, quilt, shrimp, silverware, sled, swimsuit, telephone booth, thumbtack, zero.*

3. What is the American equivalent of each of the following Briticisms? *advert, banger, bobby, chucker-out, don, draughts, dressing gown, dustbin, fortnight, hoover, plimsolls, porridge, pram, scone, spanner, starter, switchback, takeaway, telly.*

4. The *Dictionary of British Pronunciation with American Variants* shows differences in the pronunciation of 28 percent of the words therein. The broad *a* of *ahsk* and *clahss* is probably the most familiar mark of "educated" British speech, even

though the flat *a* that most Americans use is actually the older of the two pronunciations. How would a speaker with the so-called standard (or received) British accent pronounce these words? *ate, been, bone, clerk, duty, either, evolution, fear, figure, garage, herb, laboratory, leisure, lieutenant, missile, patriot, privacy, schedule, secretary, suggest, tomato* (and *potato*), *vitamin, zebra.*

5. The writing of the two languages shows such differences in spelling that it is practically impossible to go through a single page without being made aware of the writer's nationality. The most obvious divergence is in words that end in *-or* in American but *-our* in British—*behaviour, flavour, harbour, honour, labour, odour,* and *vigour.* Perhaps you have noticed the credit that pops up in many British films: COLOUR BY TECHNICOLOR.

How would these words be spelled in British English? *airplane, aluminum, check, defense, fiber, gray, inflection, inquire, jail, jewelry, judgment, maneuver, marvelous, organization, pajamas, plow, program, specialty, spelled, story* (floor of a building), *tons, vial, whiskey.*

6. Some differences exist between British and American usage. In what form is each of the following constructions and idioms likely to appear in British English? *Japan is leading the world in exports; different from; in the hospital; living on Baker Street.*

In the *Oxford Dictionary of Slang*, editors John Simpson and John Ayto identify *slang* as "English with its sleeves rolled up, its shirttails dangling, and its shoes covered with mud."

One of the hardest working and most earthy of slangs is that of London's East End cockneys.

The word *cockney* originally meant an odd or misshapen egg. Traditionally, a cockney is anyone born within the sound of Bow Bells, the bells of Bow Church, also called St. Mary-le-Bow Church. By Victorian times, the cockney dialect had spread well beyond the tintinnabulation of those bells.

Rhyming slang was first officially recorded in the mid-nineteenth century. In a series of articles published in the *Morning Chronicle* from 1849 to 1850, Henry Mayhew called it "the new style of cadgers' cant, all done on the rhyming principle." Mayhew suggested that cockney slang originated in the language of beggars and thieves and was fabricated to baffle the police.

It is an indirect sort of slang that substitutes a rhyme for the word in mind. Thus, in *Pass the Aristotle*, the last word, as you can guess, stands for bottle. In *Be sure to get the brass tacks*, *tacks* stands for facts, leading some word sleuths to deduce cockney as the source of the cliché "Let's get down to brass tacks." It's all as plain as the I suppose on your boat race— the nose on your face.

By far the great number of such expressions substitute not a word but a phrase. *I'm going down the frog and toad*—road. *I'm going up the apples and pears*—stairs. *He's gone into the soup and gravy*—navy. *She's gone out for saint and sinner*—dinner. *She's at the near 'n' far*—bar. *He's on the off 'n' on*—John. *Would ye loik Lilian Gish, Jack the Ripper, or Kate and Sidney for Jim Skinner?* translates to "Would you like fish, kipper, or steak and kidney for dinner?"

Do you get it now, *me briny marlin*—darlin'?

The process of substitution does not stop with rhyme. In

clipped speech, the actual rhyming word is often omitted. Only the first part of the phrase is spoken, and the rhyme and the word in mind are both assumed. Thus, in *Ow ye doin', me old china?* *me old china* means my old friend: *china plate*—mate. *I'll bet you can't hardly Adam it. Adam and Eve*—believe.

For those not born within the sound of Bow Bells, here are more examples:

It's a bit peasy in here. Peas in a pot—hot.

We've got some great bargains on our tom. Foolery—jewelry.

I like me glass of pig's. Pig's ear—beer.

'Ow about a cup o' Rosy? Rosy Lea—tea.

Some geezer ain't usin' 'is loaf. Of bread—head.

I come for a spot o' tiddly. Wink—drink.

How d'ye like me new whistle? And flute—suit.

I'll pay you back when I get me greens. Greengages—wages.

Let's have a butcher's at it. Hook—look.

'E's on 'is Pat. Malone—own.

Where'dye get that luverly titfer? Tat—hat.

Sometimes the journey is a long one. *Last night Pat went out with quite a Richard* means that "Last night Pat went out with quite a woman." (*Richard the Third*—*bird*; woman). *Not on yer Nellie!* means "not on your life!" (*Nellie Duff*—*puff*; breath of life).

Blimey! 'Ere's yer chance to test yer eye and ear for cockney rhyming slang. (The parenthesized words are often omitted in actual cockney speech.) Answers appear on page 284–85.

7. What is each sentence saying in standard English?

a. *Put some army (and navy) on my beef.*

b. *My compliments to the babbling brook.*

c. *In 'is 'and 'e 'eld a lady from Bristol.*

d. *That's worth a lot o' bees (and honey).*

e. *Bring the food to the Cain (and Abel).*

f. *'Ow 'bout a game o' 'orses (and carts)?*

g. *D'ye 'ear me, or are ye Mutt and Jeff?*

h. *Conan Doyle me some potatoes for kidney punch.*

i. *I'm dead on me plates (of meat).*

j. *That's one o' me favorite ding dongs.*

k. *Ye're a flipping holy friar.*

l. *It's 'round the next Johnnie Horner.*

m. *'Ow's the trouble (and strife) and the dustbin lids?*

n. *Please pass the Uncle Fred, the stammer (and stutter), and the stand at ease.*

o. *If ye drink too many o' them apple fritters, ye'll get elephant's trunk.*

THIS AMERICAN
LANGUAGE

A DECLARATION OF
LINGUISTIC INDEPENDENCE

W hen in the course of human events it becomes necessary for a people to improvise new words to catch and crystallize the new realities of a new land; to give birth to a new vocabulary endowed with its creators' irrepressible shapes and textures and flavors; to tell tales taller and funnier than anyone else had ever thought to before; to establish a body of literature in a national grain; and to harmonize a raucous chorus of immigrant voices and regional lingoes—then this truth becomes self-evident: that a nation possesses the unalienable right to declare its linguistic independence and to spend its life and liberty in the pursuit of a voice to sing of itself in its own words.

Beginning with the Pilgrims, who struggled with Native American words such as *rahaugcum* and *otchock* and transmuted them into *raccoon* and *woodchuck*, the story of language in America is the story of our Declaration of Linguistic Independence, the separating from its parent of that magnificent upstart we call American English.

John Adams was one of the first to lead the charge for American linguistic autonomy. In 1780, sixteen years before he became president, he called upon Congress to establish an academy for "correcting, improving and ascertaining the English language. . . ." "English," Adams proclaimed, "is destined to be in the next and succeeding centuries more generally the language of the world than Latin was in the last or French is in the present age."

At the time Adams made that prediction, an obscure Connecticut schoolmaster was soon to become a one-man academy of American English. His name, now synonymous with *dictionary*, was Webster. Noah Webster saw the untapped promise of the new republic. He was afire with the conviction that a United States no longer dependent on England politically should also become independent in language. In his *Dissertations on the English Language*, published in 1789, Webster declared linguistic war on the King's English: "As an independent nation, our honor requires us to have a system of our own, in language as well as government. Great Britain, whose children we are, and whose language we speak, should no longer be our standard; for the taste of her writers is already corrupted, and her language on the decline."

In putting this theory into practice, Noah Webster traveled throughout the East and the South, listening to the speech of American people and taking endless notes. He included in his dictionaries an array of shiny new American words, among them *applesauce, bullfrog, chowder, handy, hickory, succotash, tomahawk*—and *skunk:* "a quadruped remarkable for its smell." Webster also proudly used quotations by Americans to illustrate and clarify many of his definitions. The likes of Ben Franklin, George Washington, John Jay, and Washington

Irving took their places as authorities alongside William Shakespeare, John Milton, and the Bible. In shaping the American language, Webster also taught a new nation a new way to spell. He deleted the *u* from words such as *honour* and *labour* and the *k* from words such as *musick* and *publick*, he reversed the last two letters in words such as *centre* and *theatre*, and he Americanized the spelling of words such as *plough* and *gaol*.

In an 1813 letter, Thomas Jefferson echoed Webster and predicted that the vibrant young nation would need many new words. "Certainly so great growing a population," he wrote, "spread over such an extent of country, with such a variety of climates, of productions, of arts, must enlarge their language, to make it answer its purpose of expressing all ideas.... The new circumstances under which we are placed call for new words, new phrases, and for the transfer of old words to new objects. An American dialect will therefore be formed."

Perhaps no one has celebrated this "American dialect" with more passion and vigor than the poet Walt Whitman. "The Americans are going to be the most fluent and melodious-voiced people in the world—and the most perfect users of words," he jubilated before the Civil War. "The new world, the new times, the new people, the new vistas need a new tongue according—yes, what is more, they will have such a new tongue—will not be satisfied until it is evolved."

More than a century later, it's debatable whether Americans are "the most fluent and melodious-voiced people in the world," but there is no question that we are still engaged in the American Evolution and that our American parlance is as rollicking and pyrotechnic as ever. Consider our invention, in the past fifty years, of delectables on the order of *couch potato*, *mouse potato* (a couch potato attached to a computer), *digerati*, *dot-commer*, *hottie*, *humongous*, *slam dunk*, *sleazebag*, and *soccer mom*.

From the Age of Queen Anne, the British have thundered against what one of their magazines called "the torrent of barbarous phraseology" that poured from the new republic. The first British broadside launched against an Americanism is recorded in 1744, when an English visitor named Francis Moore referred to the young city of Savannah as standing upon a hill overlooking a river "which they in barbarous English call a bluff."

In general, the British beat their breasts over what *The Monthly Mirror* called "the corruptions and barbarisms which are hourly obtaining in the speech of our trans-Atlantic colonies," long after we were colonies. They objected to almost every term they did not consider standard English, protesting President Jefferson's use of the verb *belittle*. They expressed shock at the American tendency to employ, in place of *suppose*, the likes of *expect*, *reckon*, *calculate*, and—a special target—*guess*, conveniently overlooking Geoffrey Chaucer's centuries-old "Of twenty yeer of age he was, I gesse."

The acidulous British traveler Mrs. Frances Trollope scoffed in her *Domestic Manners of the Americans* (1832): "I very seldom, during my whole stay in the country, heard a sentence elegantly turned and correctly pronounced from the lips of an American. There is something either in the expression or the accent that jars the feelings and shocks the taste."

Returning from a tour through the United States later in the nineteenth century, the playwright Oscar Wilde sneered, "We really have everything in common with America nowadays except, of course, language." Wilde's fellow playwright George Bernard Shaw quipped, "England and America are two countries separated by a common language." But our home-grown treasure, Mark Twain, put it all into perspective when he quipped about American English, as compared with British English, "The property has gone into the hands of a joint stock company, and we own the bulk of the shares." Or as the great observer of the American language, H. L. Mencken, put it, "When two-thirds of the people who use a certain language decide to call it a freight train instead of a goods train, the first is correct usage, and the second is a dialect."

TALKING TURKEY

As the (probably apocryphal) tale spins out, back in the early colonial days, a white hunter and a friendly Native American made a pact before they started out on the day's hunt. Whatever they bagged was to be divided equally between them. At the end of the day, the white man undertook to distribute the spoils, consisting of several buzzards and turkeys. He suggested to his cohunter, "Either I take the turkeys and you the buzzards, or you take the buzzards and I take the turkeys." At this point the Native American complained, "You talk buzzard to me. Now talk turkey." And ever since, *to talk turkey* has meant "to tell it like it is."

Let's talk turkey about our Native American heritage. Suppose you had been one of the early explorers or settlers of North America. You would have found many things in your new land unknown to you. The handiest way of filling voids in your vocabulary would have been to ask local Native Americans what words they used. The early colonists began borrowing words from friendly Native Americans almost from the moment of their first contact, and many of those names have remained in our everyday language:

Food: *squash* (Natick), *pecan* (Algonquian), *hominy* (Algonquian), *pone* (Algonquian), *pemmican* (Cree), *succotash* (Narraganset);

People: *sachem* (Narraganset), *squaw* (Massachuset), *papoose* (Narraganset), *mugwump* (Natick);

Native American life: *moccasin* (Chippewa), *toboggan* (Algonquian), *tomahawk* (Algonquian), *wigwam* (Abenaki), *tepee* (Dakota), *caucus* (Algonquian), *pow-wow* (Narraganset), *wampum* (Massachuset), *bayou* (Choctaw), *potlatch* (Chinook), *hogan* (Navajo), *hickory* (Algonquian), *kayak* (Inuit), *totem* (Ojibwa).

Pronouncing many of the Native American words was difficult for the early explorers and settlers. In many instances, they had to shorten and simplify the names. Given the Native American names, identify the following animals:

apossoun (Don't play dead now.)

otchock (How much wood?)

rahaugcum (Ring around the tail.)

segankw (What's black and white and stinks all over?)

The hidden animals are: *opossum* (Algonquian), *woodchuck* (Narraganset), *raccoon* (Algonquian), and *skunk* (Algonquian). To this menagerie we may add the likes of *caribou* (Micmac), *chipmunk* (Ojibwa), *moose* (Algonquian), *muskrat* (Abenaki), and *porgy* (Algonquian).

If you look at a map of the United States, you will realize
how freely settlers used words of Indian origin to name the
places where we live. Rivers, lakes, ponds, creeks, mountains,
valleys, counties, towns, and cities as large as Chicago (from
a Fox word that means "place that stinks of onions" or from
another Indian word that means "great, powerful") bear Native American names, even when all or most of the speakers
of the languages have long since vanished. Four of our five
Great Lakes and twenty-five—exactly half—of our states have
names that were borrowed from Native American words:

Alabama: name of a tribe in the Creek Confederacy;
Alaska: mainland (Aleutian); *Arizona:* place of the little
springs (Papago); *Arkansas:* downstream people (Sioux); *Connecticut:* place of the long river (Algonquian);

Idaho: behold the sun coming down the mountains (Sho-
shone); *Illinois:* superior people (Illini); *Iowa:* beautiful land
(Ioway); *Kansas:* south wind people (Sioux); *Kentucky:*
meadowland (Cherokee);

Massachusetts: great hill place (Massachuset); *Michigan:*
great water (Chippewa); *Minnesota:* milky blue water (Sioux);
Mississippi: father of waters (Ojibwa); *Missouri:* people of the
large canoes (Fox);

Nebraska: flat water (Sioux); *North Dakota* and *South Dakota:* named for the Dakota tribe; *Ohio:* great river (Iroquois);
Oklahoma: red people (Choctaw);

Tennessee: name of Cherokee village; *Texas:* friends (Te-
jas); *Utah:* name of Ute tribe; *Wisconsin:* gathering of waters
(Algonquian); *Wyoming:* large prairie place (Delaware).

Some of our loveliest place names began life as Native
American words—*Susquehanna, Shenandoah, Rappahannock.*
Such names are the stuff of poetry. William Penn wrote: "I

know not a language spoken in Europe that hath words of more sweetness and greatness." To Walt Whitman, *Mononga-hela* "rolls with venison richness upon the palate." How unhappy it is that the poetry the First Peoples heard in the American landscape has eluded those who have overrun them.

ALL-AMERICAN DIALECTS

I have tongue and will travel, so I run around the country speaking to groups of teachers, students, librarians, women's clubbers, guild professionals, and corporate clients. These good people go to all the trouble of putting together meetings and conferences, and I walk in, share my thoughts about language in their lives, and imbibe their collective energy and synergy. I will go anywhere to spread the word about words, and in going anywhere from California to the New York Island, from the redwood forest to the Gulf Stream waters, I hear America singing. We are teeming nations within a nation, a nation that is like a world. We talk in melodies of infinite variety; we dance to their sundry measures and lyrics.

Midway through John Steinbeck's epic novel *The Grapes of Wrath*, young Ivy observes, "Ever'body says words different. Arkansas folks says 'em different, and Oklahomy folks says 'em different. And we seen a lady from Massachusetts, an' she said 'em differentest of all. Couldn't hardly make out what she was sayin'."

One aspect of American rugged individualism is that not all of us say the same word in the same way. Sometimes we don't even use the same name for the same object.

I was born and grew up in Philadelphia a coon's age, a blue moon, and a month of Sundays ago—when Hector was a pup. *Phillufia*, or *Philly*, which is what we kids called the city, was where the epicurean delight made with cold cuts, cheese, tomatoes, pickles, and onions stuffed into long, hard-crusted Italian bread was invented.

The creation of that sandwich took place in the Italian pushcart section of the city, known as Hog Island. Some linguists contend that it was but a short leap from *Hog Island* to *hoagie*, while others claim that the label *hoagie* arose because only a hog had the appetite or the technique to eat one properly.

As a young adult I moved to northern New England (*N'Hampsha*, to be specific), where the same sandwich designed to be a meal in itself is called a *grinder*—because you need a good set of grinders to chew them. But my travels around the United States have revealed that the hoagie or grinder is called at least a dozen other names—a bomber, Garibaldi (after the Italian liberator), hero, Italian sandwich, rocket, sub, submarine (which is what they call it in California, where I now live), torpedo, wedge, wedgie, and, in New Orleans, a po'boy (short for "poor boy").

In Philadelphia, we washed our hoagies down with soda. In New England, we did it with tonic, and by that word I don't mean medicine. Soda and tonic in other parts are known as pop, soda pop, a soft drink, Coke, quinine water, and dope.

In northern New England, they take the term *milk shake* quite literally. To many residing in that little corner of the country, a milk shake consists of milk mixed with flavored syrup—and nothing more—shaken up until foamy. If you live in Rhode Island or in southern Massachusetts and you want ice cream in your milk drink, you ask for a cabinet (named after the square wooden cabinet in which the mixer was encased). If you live farther north, you order a velvet or a frappé (from the French *frapper*, "to ice").

Clear—or is it clean?—or is it plumb?—across the nation, Americans sure do talk "different."

What do you call those flat, doughy things you often eat for breakfast—battercakes, flannel cakes, flapjacks, fritters, griddle cakes, or pancakes?

Is that simple strip of grass between the street and the sidewalk a berm, boulevard, boulevard strip, city strip, devil strip, green belt, the parking, the parking strip, parkway, sidewalk plot, strip, swale, tree bank, or tree lawn?

Is the part of the highway that separates the northbound lanes from the southbound lanes the centerline, center strip, mall, medial strip, median strip, medium strip, or neutral ground?

Is it a cock horse, dandle, hicky horse, horse, horse tilt, ridy horse, seesaw, teeter, teeterboard, teetering board, teetering horse, teeter-totter, tilt, tilting board, tinter, tinter board, or tippity bounce?

Do fisherpersons employ an angledog, angleworm, baitworm, eaceworm, earthworm, fishworm, mudworm, rainworm, or redworm? Is a larger worm a dew worm, night crawler, night walker, or town worm?

Is it a clawfish, crabfish, craw, crawdab, crawdad, crawdaddy, crawfish, crawler, crayfish, creekcrab, crowfish, freshwater lobster, ghost shrimp, mudbug, spiny lobster, or yabby?

Depends where you live and who or whom it is you're talking to.

I figger, figure, guess, imagine, opine, reckon, and suspect that my being bullheaded, contrary, headstrong, muley, mulish, ornery, otsny, pigheaded, set, sot, stubborn, or utsy about this whole matter of dialects makes you sick to, in, or at your stomach.

But I assure you that, when it comes to American dialects, I'm not speaking fahdoodle, flumaddiddle, flummydiddle, or flurriddiddle—translation: nonsense. I'm no all-thumbs-and-no-fingers, all-knees-and-elbows, all-left-feet, antigoddling, bumfuzzled, discombobulated, flusterated, or foozled bumpkin, clodhopper, country jake, hayseed, hick, hillbilly, hoosier, jack-pine savage, mossback, mountain-boomer, pumpkin-husker, rail-splitter, rube, sodbuster, stump farmer, swamp angel, yahoo, or yokel.

The biblical Book of Judges (12:4–6) tells us how one group of speakers used the word *shibboleth*, Hebrew for "stream," as a military password. The Gileadites had defeated the Ephraimites in battle and were holding some narrow places on the Jordan River that the fleeing Ephraimites had to cross to get home. In those days it was hard to tell one kind of soldier from another because soldiers didn't wear uniforms.

The Gileadites knew that the Ephraimites spoke a slightly different dialect of Hebrew and could be recognized by their inability to pronounce an initial *sh* sound. Thus, each time a soldier wanted to cross the river, "the men of Gilead said unto him, Art thou an Ephraimite? If he said, Nay, then they said unto him, Say now Shibboleth: and he said Sibboleth: for he could not frame to pronounce it right. Then they took him and slew him at the passages of Jordan: and there fell at that time of the Ephraimites forty and two thousand."

During World War II, some American officers adapted the

strategy of the Old Testament Gileadites. Knowing that many Japanese have difficulty pronouncing the letter *l*, these officers instructed their sentries to use only passwords that had *l*'s in them, such as *lallapalooza*. The closest the Japanese got to the sentries was *rarraparooza*.

These days English speakers don't get slaughtered for pronouncing their words differently from other English speakers, but the way those words sound can be labeled "funny" or "quaint" or "out of touch." In George Bernard Shaw's play *Pygmalion*, Professor Henry Higgins rails at Liza Doolittle and her cockney accent: "A woman who utters such depressing and disgusting sounds has no right to be anywhere—no right to live. Remember that you are a human being with a soul and the divine gift of articulate speech: that your native language is the language of Shakespeare and Milton and the Bible; and don't sit there crooning like a bilious pigeon!"

Most of us are aware that large numbers of people in the United States speak very differently than we do. Most of us tend to feel that the way "we" talk is right, and the way "they" talk is funny. "They," of course, refers to anyone who differs from "us."

If you ask most adults what a dialect is, they will tell you it is what somebody else in another region passes off as English. These regions tend to be exotic places like Mississippi or Texas—or Brooklyn, where *oil* is a rank of nobility and *earl* is a black, sticky substance.

It is reported that many southerners reacted to the elections of Jimmy Carter and Bill Clinton by saying, "Well, at last we have a president who talks without an accent." Actually, southerners, like everyone else, do speak with an accent, as witness these tongue-in-cheek entries in our *Dictionary of Southernisms*:

ah: organ for seeing

are: sixty minutes

arn: ferrous metal

ass: frozen water

ast: questioned

bane: small, kidney-shaped vegetable

bar: seek and receive a loan; grizzly

bold: heated in water

card: one who lacks courage

farst: a lot of trees

fur: distance

har: to employ

hep: to assist

hire yew: a greeting

paw tree: verse

rat: opposite of *lef*

reckanize: to see

tarred: exhausted

thang: item

thank: to cogitate

t'mar: day following *t'day*

Any glossary of Southernspeak would be incomplete without "*yawl:* a bunch of you's." When I visited Alexandria, Louisiana, a local pastor offered me proof that y'*all* has biblical origins, especially in the letters of the apostle Paul: "We give thanks to God always for you all, making mention of you in our prayers" (First Epistle to the Thessalonians, 1:2) and "First, I thank my God through Jesus Christ for you all" (First Epistle to the Romans, 1:8). "Obviously," the good reverend told me, "Saint Paul was a southerner." Then he added, "Thank you, Yankee visitor, for appreciating our beloved Southernspeak. We couldn't talk without it!"

An anonymous poem that I came upon in Louisville, Kentucky, clarifies the plural use of the one-syllable pronoun y'*all:*

> *Y'all gather 'round from far and near,*
> *Both city folk and rural,*
> *And listen while I tell you this:*
> *The pronoun y'all is plural.*
>
> *If I should utter, "Y'all come down,*
> *Or we-all shall be lonely,"*

I mean at least a couple folks,
And not one person only.

If I should say to Hiram Jones,
"I think that y'all are lazy,"
Or "Will y'all let me use y'all's knife?"
He'd think that I was crazy.

Don't think I mean to criticize
Or that I'm full of gall,
But when we speak of one alone,
We all say "you," not "y'all."

If the truth about dialects be told, we all have accents. Many New Englanders drop the *r*'s in *cart* and *farm* and say *caht* and *fahm*. Thus, the midwesterner's "park the car in Harvard Yard" becomes the New Englander's *pahk the cah in Hahvahd Yahd*. But those *r*'s aren't lost. A number of upper northeasterners, including the famous Kennedy family of Massachusetts, add *r*'s to words, such as *idear* and *Cuber* when those words come before a vowel or at the end of a sentence.

When an amnesia victim appeared at a truck stop in Missouri in the fall of 1987, authorities tried in vain to help her discover her identity. Even after three months, police "ran into a brick wall," according to the *Columbia Daily Tribune*. Then linguist Donald Lance of the University of Missouri-Columbia was called in to analyze her speech. After only a few sentences, Lance recognized the woman's west Pennsylvania dialect, and, within one month, police in Pittsburgh located the woman's family.

Among the clues used to pinpoint the woman's origin was the west Pennsylvanian use of *greezy* instead of *greacey*, and

teeter-totter rather than *seesaw*. Dialectologists know that people who pronounce the word as *greezy* usually live south of a
line that wiggles across the northern parts of New Jersey,
Pennsylvania, Ohio, Indiana, and Illinois.

Linguist Roger Shuy writes about the reactions of Illinois
residents in a 1962 survey of regional pronunciations, including the soundings of *greasy:* "The northern Illinois informants
felt the southern pronunciation was crude and ugly; it made
them think of a very messy, dirty, sticky, smelly frying pan. To
the southern and midland speakers, however, the northern
pronunciation connoted a messy, dirty, sticky, smelly skillet."

Using the tools of his trade, Shuy was able to accurately
profile Ted Kaczynski, the elusive Unabomber who terrorized
the nation through the 1990s. Culling linguistic evidence from
Kaczynski's "manifesto," published in the *New York Times*, and
the notes and letters accompanying the bombs, Shuy deduced
the Unabomber's geographical origin, religious background,
age, and education level.

Among the clues were the Unabomber's use of *sierras* to
mean "mountains," an indication that the writer had spent
some time living in northern California. In his "manifesto,"
Kaczynski used expressions common to a person who was a
young adult in the 1960s—*Holy Robots, working stiff,* and *playing footsy*. His employment of sociological terms, such as *other
directed,* and his many references to individual *drives* suggested
an acquaintance with the sociology in vogue during the sixties,
particularly that of David Reisman. The complexity of Kaczynski's sentence structure, including the subjunctive mood,
and the learnedness of his vocabulary, such as the words *surrogate, sublimate, overspecialization,* and *tautology*, pointed to
someone highly educated.

All these conclusions were verified when Kaczynski was

captured: He was in his early fifties, he had grown up in Chicago, he had lived for a time in northern California, and he was well educated, having once been a university professor.

Now is the time to face the fact that you speak a dialect. When you learned language, you learned it as a dialect; if you don't speak a dialect, you don't speak. *Dialect* isn't a label for careless, unlettered, nonstandard speech. A dialect isn't something to be avoided or cured.

Each language is a great pie. Each slice of that pie is a dialect, and no single slice is the language. Don't try to change your language into the kind of English that nobody really speaks. Be proud of your slice of the pie.

In the early 1960s, Steinbeck decided to rediscover America in a camper with his French poodle Charley. The writer reported his observations in a book called *Travels with Charley*, and included these thoughts on American dialects:

> One of my purposes was to listen, to hear speech, accent, speech rhythms, overtones and emphasis. For speech is so much more than words and sentences. I did listen everywhere. It seemed to me that regional speech is in the process of disappearing, not gone but going. Forty years of radio and twenty years of television must have this impact. Communications must destroy localness, by a slow, inevitable process. I can remember a time when I could almost pinpoint a man's place of origin by his speech. That is growing more difficult now and will in some foreseeable future become impossible. It is a rare house or building that is not rigged with spiky combers of the air. Radio and television speech becomes standardized, perhaps better English than we have ever used. Just as our bread, mixed and baked, packaged and sold without

benefit of accident or human frailty, is uniformly good and uniformly tasteless, so will our speech become one speech.

Forty years have passed since Steinbeck made that observation, and the hum and buzz of electronic voices have since permeated almost every home across our nation. Formerly, the psalmist tells us, "the voice of the turtle was heard in the land," but now it is the voice of the broadcaster, with his or her immaculately groomed diction. I hope that American English does not turn into a bland, homogenized, pasteurized, assembly line product. May our bodacious American English remain tasty and nourishing—full of flavor, variety, and local ingredients.

SLANG AS IT IS SLUNG

Slang is hot and slang is cool. Slang is nifty and slang is wicked. Slang is the bee's knees, the cat's whiskers, and the cat's pajamas. Slang is far out, groovy, and outta sight. Slang is fresh, fly, and phat. Slang is bodacious, ducky, and fantabulous. Slang is ace, awesome, bad, sweet, smooth, co-pacetic, the most, the max, and totally tubular.

Those are twenty-five ways of saying that, if variety is the spice of life, slang is the spice of language. Slang adds gusto to the feast of words, as long as speakers and writers remember that too much spice can kill the feast of any dish.

What is slang? In the preface to their *Dictionary of American Slang*, Harold Wentworth and Stuart Berg Flexner define slang as "the body of words and expressions frequently used by or intelligible to a rather large portion of the general American public, but not accepted as good, formal usage by the majority." Slang, then, is seen as a kind of vagabond language that prowls the outskirts of respectable speech, yet few of us can get along without it. Even our statespersons have a hard time getting by without such colloquial or slang expressions as *hit the nail on the head, team effort, pass the buck,* and *talk turkey.*

Nobody is quite sure where the word *slang* comes from. According to H. L. Mencken, *slang* developed in the eighteenth century (it was first recorded in 1756) either from an erroneous past tense of *sling (sling-slang-slung)* or from the word *language* itself, as in (thieve)*s'lang*(uage) and (beggar)*s'-lang*(uage). The second theory makes the point that jargon and slang originate and are used by a particular trade or class group, but slang words come to be slung around to some extent by a whole population.

The use of slang is far more ancient than the word *slang* itself. In fact, slang is nearly as old as language itself, and in all languages at all times some slang expressions have entered the mainstream of the vocabulary to pollute or enrich, depending on one's view of the matter. We find traces of slang in the Sanskrit of ancient India, where writers amused themselves now and then by calling a *head* a "dish." In Latin literary records we discover, alongside *caput,* the standard term for "head," the word *testa,* which meant "pot" or "jug." Both the Sanskrit "dish" and the Latin "pot" share the flavor of our modern *crackpot, jughead,* and *mug.*

The fourteenth-century poet Geoffrey Chaucer used *gab* for "talk" and *bones* for "dice," exactly as we employ them today. William Shakespeare, the literary lord of stage and classroom, coined *costard* (a large apple) to mean "head" and *clay-brained* and *knotty pated* to mean "slow of wit." We discover "laugh yourself into stitches" in *Twelfth Night,* "not so hot" in *The Winter's Tale,* and "right on" in *Julius Caesar.*

There are some very human reasons why the river of slang courses through every language. One of them is that people like novelty and variety in their lives and in their language.

To satisfy this urge, they continuously coin new slang words and expressions. This disquisition began with twenty-five breezy ways of saying "wonderful," but that feat pales next to the 2,231 synonyms for *drunk* (and fifty pages' worth) that Paul Dickson trots out in his book *Words*—from the euphemistic *tired* to the comical *plastered*, from the terminal *stiff* to the uncategorizable *zoozled*.

Second, slang allows us to break the ice and shift into a more casual and friendly gear. "What's cooking?" or "How's it going?" sound more easygoing and familiar than "How do you do?" "Slang," said Carl Sandburg, is "language that rolls up its sleeves, spits on its hands, and gets to work."

A third motive is sheer playfulness. Slang such as *rubbernecker* for a sightseer in a car and *motormouth* for someone who gabs on and on and reduplications such as *heebie-jeebies* and *okeydokey* tickle our sense of humor.

Finally, as G. K. Chesterton proclaimed, "All slang is metaphor, and all metaphor is poetry." American slang abounds in fresh figures of speech that evoke arresting word pictures in the mind's eye. We intellectually understand "an angry, persecuted husband," but the slanguage version "a henpecked husband stewing in his own juice" takes a vivid shortcut to our imagination.

An English professor announced to the class, "There are two words I don't allow in my class. One is *gross* and the other is *cool*." From the back of the room a voice called out, "So what are the two words?" Slang is a powerful stimulant that keeps our American language alive and growing. Slang is a prominent part of our American wordscape. In fact, the *Dictionary of American Slang* estimates that slang makes up perhaps a fifth of the words we use. Many of our most valuable and pungent words have begun their lives keeping company with thieves, vagrants, and hipsters. As Mr. Dooley, a fictional saloon keeper, once observed, "When we Americans get through with the English language, it will look as if it has been run over by a musical comedy."

FAREWELL TO THE OKAY MAN

On October 16, 2002, Allen Walker Read, a playful prospector of the American tongue, died at his home in Manhattan. He was ninety-six. A long-time professor at Columbia University, Read was the word detective who traced the word *Dixie* to an 1850 minstrel show, the word *Podunk* to an Indian name meaning "a swamp" or "a sinking," and *the almighty dollar* to the American author Washington Irving.

But he was best known for having hunted down the origin of *OK*, perhaps the most useful expression of universal communication ever devised. *OK* is recognizable and pronounceable in almost every language on earth. *OK* is so protean that it can function as five parts of speech—noun: "I gave it my OK"; verb: "I'll OK it"; adjective: "He's an OK guy"; adverb: "She sings OK"; and interjection: "OK, let's party!"

The explanations for the origin of *OK* have been as imaginative as they have been various. But Professor Read proved that *OK* did not derive from *okeh*, an affirmative reply in Choctaw; nor from the name of chief Old Keokuk; nor from a fellow named Orrin Kendall, who manufactured a tasty brand of army biscuit for Union soldiers in the Civil War; nor from the Haitian port Aux Cayes, which produced superior rum; nor from *open key*, a telegraph term; nor from the Greek *olla kalla*, "all good."

Rather, as Read pointed out in a series of articles in *American Speech*, 1963–64, the truth is more politically correct than any of these theories. He tracked down the first known published appearance of *OK* with its current meaning in the Boston *Morning Post* on March 23, 1839. Here—ta da!—is the world's very first printed *OK*:

"The 'Chairman of the Committee on Charity Lecture Bells' is one of the deputation, and perhaps if he should return to Boston, via Providence, he of the Journal, and his trainband, would have the 'contribution box,' et ceteras, o.k.—all correct—and cause the corks to fly, like sparks, upward."

Allen Walker Read demonstrated that *OK* started life as an obscure joke and through a twist of fate went to the top of the charts on the American hit parade of words. In the 1830s, in New England, there was a craze for initialisms, in the manner of *FYI*, *PDQ*, *aka*, and *TGIF*, so popular today. The fad went so far as to generate letter combinations of intentionally comic misspellings: *KG* for "know go," *KY* for "know yuse," *NSMJ* for " 'nough said 'mong gentlemen," and *OR* for "oll rong." *OK* for "oll korrect" naturally followed.

Of all those loopy initialisms and facetious misspellings, *OK* alone survived. That's because of a presidential nickname that consolidated the letters in the national memory. Martin Van Buren, elected our eighth president in 1836, was born in Kinderhook, New York, and, early in his political career, was dubbed "Old Kinderhook." Echoing the "Oll Korrect" initialism, *OK* became the rallying cry of the Old Kinderhook Club, a Democratic organization supporting Van Buren during the 1840 campaign. Thus, the accident of Van Buren's birthplace rescued *OK* from the dustbin of history.

The coinage did Van Buren no good, and he was defeated in his bid for reelection. But the word honoring his name today remains what H. L. Mencken identified as "the most shining and successful Americanism ever invented."

Mencken also wrote, in 1948, that "Allen Walker Read probably knows more about early Americanisms than anyone else on earth." All of us wordaholics, logolepts, lexicomanes, and verbivores are grateful to Dr. Read for his loving labors in the language vineyards. We wish him happy word hunting forevermore.

THE CIRCUS OF WORDS

"H ey, First-of-May! Tell the butcher in the backyard to stay away from the bulls, humps, stripes, and painted ponies. We have some cherry pie for him before doors and spec."

Sound like double-talk? Actually, it's circus talk—or, more technically, circus argot, argot being a specialized vocabulary used by a particular group for mutual bonding and private communication.

First-of-May designates anyone who is brand-new to circus work. That's because circuses used to start their tours around the first day in May. A *butcher* is a concessionaire who sells cotton candy (*floss*) and other food, along with drinks and souvenirs, to the audience during the show. The *backyard* is the place just behind the circus entrance where performers wait to do their acts. A *bull* is a circus elephant, even though most of them are female. Among other circus beasts, *humps*, *stripes*, and *painted ponies* are, respectively, camels, tigers, and zebras. *Cherry pie* is extra work, probably from *chairy pie*, the setting up of extra chairs around the arena. *Doors!* is the cry

69

that tells circus folk that the audience is coming in to take their seats, and *spec* is short for *spectacle*, the big parade in which all performers take part.

Trust me: This topic ain't no *dog and pony show*—the designation for a small circus with just a few acts, also known as a *mud show*.

During a fund drive for WNYC public radio, I fielded questions from New York's finest listeners. At some point, host Leonard Lopate pitched this line: "It costs this station almost $700,000 a year to buy all the national programs you hear each weekend. That's a really big nut to make."

Sure enough, a listener called in to ask the origin of *making the nut*. I love questions like that because I get my audio radiance from my radio audience, and I explained to the listener that when a circus came to town, the sheriff would often remove the nut from a wheel of the main wagon. Because in bygone days these nuts were elaborate and individually crafted, they were well nigh impossible to replace. Thus, the circus couldn't leave town until the costs of land and utilities rental, easements, and security were paid. It's but a short metaphorical leap to the modern meaning of *making the nut*, "meeting one's expenses."

Communities are most likely to develop a colorful argot when they have limited contact with the world outside of their group. The circus community is a perfect example of the almost monastic self-containment in which argot flourishes. Big Top people travel in very close quarters; and because they usually go into a town, set up, do a show, tear down, and leave, they have little contact with the locals. They socialize with each other, they intermarry, and their children acquire the argot from the time they start to talk.

They quickly learn that what we call the toilet is the *don-*

niker, the place where circus people can get snacks is a *grease joint,* and a circus performer is a *kinker.* The townspeople are *towners* or *rubes.* In the old days, large groups of towners who believed (sometimes accurately) they had been fleeced by dishonest circus people would come back in a mob for revenge. The cry *Hey Rube!* went out, and everyone knew that the fight was on.

A full house is called a *straw house* from the days when straw would be laid down in front of the seats to accommodate more people than the seats could hold. Distances between engagements were called *jumps.* Thus, an old circus toast rings out: "May your lots be grassy, your jumps short, and your houses straw."

STAMP OUT FADSPEAK!

Some people lament that speaking and writing these days are simply a collection of faddish clichés patched together like the sections of prefabricated houses made of ticky-tacky. They see modern discourse as a mindless clacking of trendy expressions, many of them from movies and television sitcoms.

Why is English discourse in such a parlous state? Maybe it's because verbal knee-jerkery requires no thought. It's so much easier not to think, isn't it? It's so much easier to cookie-cut the rich dough of the English language. It's so much easier to microwave a frozen dinner than to create a meal from scratch. After all, when we were children, we loved to pull the string on the doll that said the same thing over and over, again and again.

That's what fadspeak is—the unrelenting mix of mimicry and gimmickry. Fadspeak comprises vogue phrases that suddenly appear on everybody's tongues—phrases that launch a thousand lips. Before you can say, "yada yada yada," these throwaway expressions become instant clichés, perfect for our throwaway society, like paper wedding dresses for throwaway marriages. Fadspeak clichés lead mayfly lives, counting their duration in months instead of decades. They strut and fret their hour upon the stage of pop culture and then are heard no more.

Now, would I, your faithful, deep pockets, drop-dead-good-looking language columnist, your poster boy for user-friendly writing, ever serve you anything totally bogus like fadspeak? I don't think so. Not a problem. I have zero tolerance for anything that lowers the bar for what makes world-class writing.

Work with me on this. I've been around the block, and I know a thing or two. I know that I wear many hats, but I'm not talking trash here. I'm not the eight-hundred-pound gorilla out to bust your chops. I feel your pain, and I'm your new best friend. At this point in time, I've got you on my radar screen, and I know you da man! Yessss!

Hey, people, this isn't rocket science or brain surgery. Call me crazy, but it's simply a no-brainer—a drop kick and a slam dunk. I, the mother of all language writers, will go to the mat 24–7 for fresh, original language. You know what? I'm my own toughest critic, so I get more bang for the buck when I avoid those new clichés. I want to level the playing field and give something back to the community. Join the club. Do the math. Get used to it. It works for me. Welcome to my world.

So I'm making you an offer you can't refuse. Maybe it's more than you want to know, but I'm never going to slip into those hackneyed faddish expressions that afflict our precious American language. Having said that, how about we run that one up the flagpole and see who salutes? Sound like a plan? It's a done deal because I've got a full plate, and I bring a lot to the table. I come to play, and the ball's in your court.

Sheesh. Get over it. Doesn't it yank your chain and rattle your cage when a writer or speaker puts dynamite language on the back burner? Doesn't it send you on an emotional roller-coaster until you crash and burn when they try to put a good face on it? Doesn't fadspeak just blow you out of the water and make you want to scream, "Oh, puh-leeze! In your dreams! Excuuuuse me! It's my way or the highway! Why are you shooting yourself in the foot? You're history! You're toast! That's so twentieth century! Put a sock in it! Don't give up your day job!"?

As for me, I'm like, "Are you the writer from Hell? You are all over the map. You are like a deer caught in the headlights. Lose the attitude, man. You are so-o-o-o busted. Read my lips! Maybe it's a guy thing, but get real! Get an attitude adjustment. Get with the twenty-first century! Get a life! And while you're at it, why don't you knock yourself out and get a vocabulary?"

Anyhoo, off the top of my head, the bottom line is that fadspeakers and fadwriters—and you know who you are—are so clueless. I am shocked—shocked!—that they just don't suck it up, get up to speed, go the whole nine yards, push the envelope, take it to another level, and think outside the box. All they do is give you that same-old-same-old, been-there-done-that kind of writing.

Tell me about it. Fadspeakers and fadwriters just play the old tapes again and again, and their ideas just fall through the cracks. They're not playing with a full deck. The light's on, but nobody's home. Elvis has left the building. Go figure.

Hel-lo-oh? Earth to cliché meisters. Duuuh. Boooring. What's wrong with this picture? Are we on the same page? Are we having fun yet? Are you having some kind of a bad-hair day? Are you having a midlife crisis? A senior moment? Maybe it's time for a wake-up call? Or maybe a reality check? I don't think so. In your dreams. Not even close.

O-o-k-a-a-a-y. You wanna talk about it? You wanna get with the program? I feel your pain, but why don't you wake up and smell the coffee? How about we cut right to the chase? I mean, what part of "fadspeak" don't you understand? Deal with it. You got that right. Or maybe I'm just preaching to the choir.

Whatever. As if.

Now that I've got your attention, here's the buzz on viable, cutting-edge communication. Whenever I find one of these snippets of fadspeak strewn about a sentence, I'm in your face. I'm your worst nightmare. Those flavor-of-the-month phrases just make me go ballistic, even to the point of going postal. After all—and I'm not making this up—what goes around comes around.

All right. My bad. I understand that you're not a happy camper and maybe you just don't want to go there. But I do because I've got all my ducks in a row. I mean, at the end of the day, is this a great language—or what? I mean, it's a language to die for. I mean, if they can put a man on the moon, why can't they teach people to write well?

Gimme a break. Cut me some slack. What am I, chopped liver? Hey, what do I know? And now that I've thrown my hissy fit about fadspeak, here's what's going down.

Thanks a bunch for letting me share. Now that I've been able to tell it like it is, it's time to pack it in. I'm outa here. Talk to you soon. Buh-bye—and have a nice day.

LIKE, WHERE IS OUR
LANGUAGE GOING?

A woman asked a young clerk in one of the megachain bookstores who the author of *Like Water for Chocolate* was. After the salesperson had spent five minutes searching and still could not locate the famous title, the customer realized that the young man had been looking for *Water from Chocolate*.

It's like . . . you know.

Nowadays three speech patterns of the younger generation squeak like chalk across the blackboard of adult sensibilities:

- The sprinkling of *like* throughout sentences, like, you know what I'm saying?

- The use of another species of *like* as a replacement of the verb *say*: "I'm like, 'Yeah, it's like totally wicked awesome.' "

- The replacement of *say*, a verb of locution, by *go*, a verb of locomotion: "She goes, 'Hey, that video game was totally cool.' " Linguists call this use "quotative," an introduction to direct speech.

Professor Mark Hale, of the Harvard University Department of Linguistics, says of these speech markers: "This is national in scope. It is not idiosyncratic in any particular part of the country. But it is observed most often among younger people, usually younger than twenty-five."

As a trained linguist, I am fascinated by all change in language, and I don't rush to judgment. The burgeoning of *like* in American discourse appears to be a verbal tic in the linguistic mold of "uh" and "you know." It offers the speaker's thoughts an opportunity to catch up with his or her onrushing sentences or to emphasize important points. Take the statement, "I didn't hand in my book report because like the dog peed on my Cliff's Notes." Here *like* is an oral mark of crucial punctuation that indicates "important information ahead."

According to Professor Hale, increasing numbers of speakers press into service *go* and *like* for *say* as a badge of identification that proclaims, "I am a member of a certain generation and speech community."

Hmm. My professional rule of thumb is that all linguistic change is neither good nor bad but thinking makes it so. Still, the promiscuous employment of *like* and *go* stirs my concern about the state of our English language. To most of us, *like* is a preposition that means that something is similar to something else but is not the idea or thing itself. Thus, dusting statements with a word of approximation seems to me to encourage half thoughts. I fret that the permeating influence of *like* makes imprecision the norm and keeps both speakers and listeners from coming to grips with the thoughts behind the words. "I'm like a supporter of human rights" lacks the commitment of "I support human rights" because *like* leads off a simile of general likeness, not a literal statement.

I believe that it is not a coincidence that *go* and *like* as introductions to quoted speech have accompanied the burgeoning of *like* as a rhetorical qualifier. I sense a fear of commitment both to direct thought and to the act of communicating—saying and asserting one's observations and opinions. Whenever I hear a young person—or, as is increasingly the case, an older person—declare (not *go*): "She goes, 'I'm like totally committed to human rights,' " I want to say (not *I'm like*), "Where did she go, and is she really committed? Did she really mean what she said [not *went*]?"

"Language is the Rubicon that divides man from beast," declared the philologist Max Müller. The boundary between our species and the others on this planet that run and fly and creep and swim is the language line. To blur that line by replacing verbs of speaking with verbs of motion is to deny the very act that defines our kind.

I'm like it's totally uncool.

A NOO-KYUH-LUR

NONPROLIFERATION TREATISE

In a stunning *New York Times* article, Jesse Sheidlower, the North American editor of the *Oxford English Dictionary*, contends that it is now time to accept *noo-kyuh-lur* as a variant pronunciation of *noo-klee-ur*. The sounding *noo-kyuh-lur* has received much notoriety because a number of presidents from Dwight David Eisenhower to George W. Bush have sounded the word that way. Broadcaster and language commentator Edwin Newman writes: "The word, correctly pronounced, is too much for a fair part of the population, and education and experience seem to have nothing to do with it."

Noo-kyuh-lur is an example of metathesis, the transposition of sounds within a word, as in *ree-luh-tur* for Realtor, *joo-luh-ree* for jewelry, *lahr-niks* for larynx, and, more subtly *cumf-ter-bull* for comfortable. Sheidlower observes that, in addition to the pressures of metathesis, the *-ular* combination is a common pattern in English—*circular, muscular, particular, vascular,* and the like—while *-lear* is heard only in rare words such as *likelier* and *cochlear*. He argues that these patterns are evidence that the time has come to include *noo-kyuh-lur* as an acceptable sounding. In fact, the objections to *noo-kyuh-lur* are "a lost cause."

I beg—indeed demand—to differ, or as President George W. Bush has exclaimed, "Not over my dead body!" He really meant, "Over my dead body!"—and so do I. While the metathesis *cumf-ter-bull* (in which the *er* and the *t* have been transposed) is fully acceptable and entrenched in our language, cultivated speakers generally consider *noo-kyuh-lur*, *ree-luh-tur*, and their ilk atrocities. From Eisenhower (who simply "could not get it right," writes Edwin Newman) to George W. Bush,* *noo-kyuh-lur* has never stopped raising hackles and igniting jeers. The *San Diego Union-Tribune* recently polled its readers to find out the grammar and pronunciation abuses that most seismically yanked their chains and rattled their cages. *Noo-kyuh-lur* was the crime against English mentioned by the greatest number of respondents. Their comments made it clear that *noo-kyuh-lur* twisted their faces into an imitation of Edvard Munch's expressionist screamer at the bridge. *Noo-kyuh-lur* made them go ballistic, even *noo-klee-ur*. Despite its proliferation, *noo-kyuh-lur* has failed to gain respectability. *Noo-kyuh-lur* may be a sad fact of life, but resistance to it is hardly "a lost cause." Although we hear it from some prominent people, it remains a much-derided aberration.

I find three aspects of the *noo-klee-ur/noo-kyuh-lur* confusion especially scary:

First, when a prominent lexicographer of Jesse Sheidlower's stature endorses *noo-kyuh-lur* as a variant pronunciation, acceptability may not be far ahead of us.

---

*Former president Jimmy Carter, who helped Admiral Rickover develop the U.S. nuclear submarine program, has long pronounced the adjective as *noo-kee-ur*.

Second, doesn't it concern you that the man with his finger closest to the red panic button doesn't pronounce the word correctly?

And scariest of all: President Bush's advisers surely could coach him to sound the word correctly as *noo-klee-ur* ("Mr. President, the noun form is *noo-klee-us*. Now please replace the last syllable, *us*, with *ur*, as in *noo-klee-ur*.")

But apparently, the president's speech coaches have decided that his continued mispronunciation will impress us as more folksy, more connecting. Whew. Talk about the dumbing down of the American mind.

GETTING THE WORD OUT

WRITING IS . . .

For me, writing is like throwing a Frisbee.

You can play Frisbee catch with yourself, but it's repetitious and not much fun. Better it is to fling to others, to extend yourself across a distance.

At first, your tossing is awkward and strengthless. But, with time and practice and maturity, you learn to set your body and brain and heart at the proper angles, to grasp with just the right force, and not to choke the missile. You discover how to flick the release so that all things loose and wobbly snap together at just the right moment. You learn to reach out your follow-through hand to the receiver to ensure the straightness and justice of the flight.

And on the just-right days, when the sky is blue and the air pulses with perfect stillness, all points of the Frisbee spin together within their bonded circle—and the object glides on its own whirling, a whirling invisible and inaudible to all others but you.

Like playing Frisbee, writing is a re-creation-al joy. For me, a lot of the fun is knowing that readers out there—you among them—are sharing what I have made. I marvel that, as you pass your eyes over these words, you experience ideas and emotions similar to what I was thinking and feeling when, in another place and another time, I struck the symbols on my keyboard.

Like a whirling, gliding Frisbee, my work extends me beyond the frail confines of my body. Thank you for catching me.

HOW I WRITE

Ernest Hemingway's first rule for writers was to apply the seat of the pants to the seat of the chair. But not all authors are able to survive with such a simple approach.

Émile Zola pulled the shades and composed by artificial light. Francis Bacon, we are told, knelt each day before creating his greatest works. Martin Luther could not write unless his dog was lying at his feet, while Ben Jonson needed to hear his cat purring. Marcel Proust sealed out the world by lining the walls of his study with cork. Emily Dickinson hardly ever left her home and garden. Wallace Stevens composed poetry while walking to and from work each day at a Hartford insurance company. Alexander Pope and Jean Racine could not write without first declaiming at the top of their voices. Jack Kerouac began each night of writing by kneeling in prayer and composing by candlelight. Freidrich Schiller started each of his writing sessions by opening the drawer of his desk and breathing in the fumes of the rotten apples he had stashed there.

Some writers have donned and doffed gay apparel. Early in his career, John Cheever wore a business suit as he traveled from his apartment to a room in his basement. Then he hung the suit on a hanger and wrote in his underwear. Jessamyn West wrote in bed without getting dressed, as, from time to time, did Eudora Welty, Edith Wharton, Mark Twain, and Truman Capote. John McPhee worked in his bathrobe and tied its sash to the arms of his chair to keep from even thinking about deserting his writing room.

For stimulation, Honoré de Balzac wrote in a monk's costume and drank at least twenty cups of coffee a day, eventually dying of caffeine poisoning. As his vision failed, James Joyce took to wearing a milkman's uniform when he wrote, believing that its whiteness caught the sunlight and reflected it onto his pages. Victor Hugo went to the opposite lengths to ensure his daily output of words on paper. He gave all his clothes to his servant with orders that they be returned only after he had finished his day's quota.

Compared to such strategies, my daily writing regimen is drearily normal. Perhaps that's because I'm a nonfictionalist— a hunter-gatherer of language who records the sounds that escape from the holes in people's faces, leak from their pens, and luminesce on their computer screens. I don't drink coffee. Rotten fruit doesn't inspire (literally "breathe into") me. My lifelong, heels-over-head love affair with language is my natural caffeine and fructose.

To be a writer, one must behave as writers behave. They write. And write. And write. The difference between a writer and a wannabe is that a writer is someone who can't not write, while a wannabe says, "One of these days when . . . , then I'll . . . ." Unable not to write, I write every day that I'm home.

A grocer doesn't wait to be inspired to go to the store or a banker to go to the bank. I can't afford the luxury of waiting to be inspired before I go to work. Writing is my job, and it happens to be a job that almost nobody gives up on purpose. I love my job as a writer, so I write. Every day that I can.

Long ago, I discovered that I would never become the great American novelist. I stink at cobbling characters, dialogue, episode, and setting. You won't find much of that fictional stuff in my books, unless the story serves the ideas I am trying to communicate. A writer has to find out which kind of writer he or she is, and I somehow got born an English teacher with an ability to illuminate ideas about language and literature.

Jean-Jacques Rousseau wrote only in the early morning, Alain-René Lesage at midday, and Lord Byron at midnight. Early on, I also discovered that I am more lark than owl—more a morning person than a night person—and certainly not a bat, one who writes through the night. I usually hit the ground punning at around 7:30 A.M. and am banging away at the keyboard within an hour.

I write very little on paper, almost everything on my computer. My work possesses an informational density, and the computer allows me to enter all manner of matter onto the hard drive and accumulate that density. Theodore Sturgeon once wrote, "Nine-tenths of everything is crap." The computer allows me to dump crap into the hard drive without the sense of permanence that handwriting or type on paper used to signify to me. I'm visual and shape my sentences and paragraphs most dexterously on a screen. The computer has not only trebled my output. It has made me a more joyful, liberated, and better writer.

Genetic and environmental roulette have allowed me to

be able to work in a silent or a noisy environment. I'm a speaker as well as a writer, so phone calls and faxes and e-messages chirp and hum and buzz in my writing room, and I often have to answer them during those precious morning hours. That's all right with me. Fictionalists shut the world out. Fictionalists live with their imaginary characters, who get skittish and may flee a noisy room. As I cobble my essays, my readers are my companions, and they will usually stay with me in my writing space through outerworldly alarms and excursions.

Besides, the business of the writing business gives me the privilege of being a writer. In fact, I consider the writing only about half my job. Writers don't make a living writing books. They make a living selling books. After all, I do have to support my writing habit.

When you are heels over head in love with what you do, you never work a day. That's me—butt over teakettle in love with being a writer—a job that nobody who works it would give up on purpose.

A WORDY WEEKEND

T all and majestic on a mountaintop in New Paltz, New York, sits the stately, turreted Mohonk Mountain House, looking as if it belongs somewhere in the Swiss Alps rather than within a throne's stow of New York City. Set amidst the natural beauty of enormous old trees, wooded trails, glaciated rock cliffs, and a crystal blue lake, the national landmark also exudes the Victorian charm of gazebos, gatehouses, and greenhouses outside and paneled rooms, hand-carved furniture, and fireplaces inside. For the more active guests who prefer doing to seeing, Mohonk offers a succession of more than forty theme programs that include a music weekend, a mystery weekend, a comic strip weekend, and even a chocolate weekend.

It is mid-November of 1991, and I have returned to this mountaintop resort for the second time to speak at and romp through the annual Wonderful World of Words weekend. It is Friday night, and the front desk is busy checking in hotel guests, but the guests checking in are even busier. While the clerks merely have to sign in the guests and hand out the keys, the guests now have a Packet of Puzzlers, and apparently they can't wait to get started. They attack the word games in the packet even as they head for the elevators, or they sit right down in chairs nearby and start writing at once. Here is the shortest of six posers that will be served up during our wordy weekend. Give it your best before consulting "Answers to Games and Quizzes" (page 285).

Each of the following crypticlike words represents a well-known motto, phrase, or saying. For example, KDI would be the abbreviated version of "crazy, mixed-up kid," and TIME TIME would be "time and time again."

1. Busines

2. Timing tim ing

3. Rhutt fiction

4. Writiting

5. Wa ys

6. Bsoduyl

7. **Blood**water

8. Jump jump sheriff

9. I right I

10. Well enough

11. Bucdropket

12. Herbuck

Gloria Rosenthal, all five-feet-two of her, bustles about greeting regulars and welcoming newcomers. A self-described "word buff, puzzle nut, and language lover," Gloria is a Long Island writer and lecturer who is the originator, creator, co-ordinator, gamesmonger, and absolute wordmistress of the Wonderful World of Words weekend. When she is not putting this event together, creating word games for magazines and puzzle books, or writing fiction and articles, she is busy being a wife, mother, and grandmother.

Gloria's support staff for the weekend comprises her husband Larry, her sister Babe, and brother-in-law Sonny, and her daughter Amy, who has flown in from Minneapolis to help. They all wear the Wonderful World of Words sweatshirts.

When I ask Gloria to describe the typical person who attends this wordy getaway, she says, "Over the years I've discovered that a love of language does not necessarily have anything to do with one's profession or occupation. Avid word buffs come from every field. They're lawyers, doctors, teachers, retired people, secretaries, nurses, insurance brokers, salespeople, housewives, and househusbands. I knew a bridge builder, a real 'dese' and 'dose' kind of fellow, who loved language as passionately as any of us.

"There are different types of word lovers—those who play with words, those who turn a phrase, those who pop a pun, and those who solve a puzzle. It calls for a trick of the mind that has little to do with education. Someone with a passion for words sees a sign, as I once did, that says 'Laundry Palace' and immediately drops some letters to come up with 'Land Dry Place' and then keeps beheading so that *place* becomes *lace* and then *ace*. For true word lovers, even the simplest word can tickle their punnybone and get them going."

Marcia Hillman, a lyricist from Manhattan who has attended eight of the ten Wonderful World of Words weekends, tells me, "I love this stuff. I write lyrics, which means my head is forever spinning, which is why I like to do puzzles. Attending the Wonderful Weekend of Words is like going to a health spa for your brain. The whole experience is yoga for the brain cells—a joyous stretch for the mind."

Jeannia Yapczenski, a fourth-grade teacher from Carteret, New Jersey, has made the pilgrimage to New Paltz for all ten years of wordiful weekends. "I'm a wordaholic," Jeannia tells me. "I find this weekend to be therapy, and so do others. People who meet here have occasional reunions in New York throughout the year. I love the games approach to life, and I wish there were more games and puzzle books for children."

The first gathering, in the spacious, oaken main hall, is for my opening talk, "From Bard to Verse," on the mind-boggling contributions of William Shakespeare to our English tongue (including the phrase "boggles the mind"). Other speakers who have been similarly inspired to lend their talents to the Wonderful World of Words weekend include Dick Cavett, Maura Jacobson, Edwin Newman, Will Weng, Willard Espy, Thomas Middleton, Peter Funk, and Paul Dickson. I can see why. It is always a pleasure to talk to word lovers, but this eager, attentive, rollicking assemblage seems "gift rapt" for a speaker who wants to share his words about words.

After my presentation, everyone gathers for an ice-breaking game ("break the ice" is another phrase that Shakespeare bequeathed us) invented by Gloria and Larry. Scrambled SCRABBLE® is a team form of SCRABBLE® allowing up to seventy-seven gamesters to play using giant tiles. Each team forms its word collectively, holds up the tiles, and receives a score.

A casually attired fiftysomething man with a salt-and-pepper beard and a keen gleam in his eye has not joined a group but is very much caught up in the game. In a crowd you would not recognize him as Stephen Sondheim, the brilliant, award-winning composer and lyricist, but when he talks about words and puzzles, you just know that this fellow does extraordinary things with language every day of his life.

Stephen walks around the Scrambled SCRABBLE® room looking at everyone's words, obviously trying not to show approval or disapproval. At one point, clearly in considerable anguish, he rushes over to Gloria and laments, "That team has a seven-letter word and they don't know it!"

The next morning, Stephen lectures briefly about "Puzzles, Lyrics, and Other Word Games." "As a kid," he tells us, "I was always fascinated with words. Even before I could read, I could recognize songs by the length of the words. I have always seen words as collections of letters, a quirk in the head, like being double-jointed."

Most of Stephen's presentation is a question-and-answer session, and both the questions and the answers are scintillating. "To fit the meanings and syllables to the rise and fall of music is akin to constructing a crossword puzzle and fitting letters into grids," he explains. Such is this music man's fascination with creative word puzzles that we learn that *West Side Story* could have been completed two weeks earlier if Stephen and his collaborator, Leonard Bernstein, had not spent so much time working on cryptic crossword puzzles.

Mary Higgins Clark is the next Saturday morning speaker. She is a thoroughly charming and down-to-earth woman, so friendly and sharing that it's hard to imagine her sitting alone plotting and writing about murders, which she accomplishes with considerable success—if you want to call being America's most widely read suspense writer a success! She talks about "The Mystery of Words," and she enthralls her audience.

Mary explains that she "was born into an Irish family,

where words were the stuff and credence of life. How does an Irishman propose? He says, 'Would you care to be buried with me, Mother?' Words are my business," she tells us. "I started reading from the time I could interpret two words together. And I've always been a writer. I started writing from day one."

I ask Mary how she got started as a writer. "I remember being asked by my sixth-grade teacher, Sister Mary Lorenzo, to write a paragraph using all twelve spelling words of the day. Then my teacher took me around to read the paragraph to all the classes. And it made me feel wonderful." I imagine what Mary Higgins Clark must feel like today with more than 20 million of her books being read in the United States and millions more around the world.

The next weekend attraction is the Saturday afternoon Great American Will Shortz Team Treasure Hunt. At this time Will Shortz is the senior editor of *Games* magazine and puzzlemeister on National Public Radio's *Weekend Edition* but not yet the puzzle editor for the *New York Times*. He has been making up posers since he was eight and selling them to national magazines since the age of fourteen. At Indiana University, he became the first and only person to major in puzzles and to receive, in 1974, a degree in enigmatology, the art and science of puzzle construction.

"I love to whack people on the side of the head and make them see words and language in a new way," Will explains to me. "Most people's jobs are not creative. They don't use their minds in fresh ways. By solving puzzles, they gain the pleasure of being creative."

Since the Wonderful World of Words weekend began in 1982, Will has been program leader and created and run the treasure hunt. The challenge is a tantalizing sequence of puzzles wherein teams must solve one enigma to get the clue to solve another enigma to get a clue, and so on. Contestants are rushing all over the hotel, up and down the stairs, in and out of public places, such as the gift shop, where magazines have been fanned out so that the initial letters of each title subtly spell out the acrostic PIANO IN TV ROOM. Prizes for winners of all weekend competitions are games and books, but from the zeal and zest of the players you would think that the big payoff is, at the very least, a trip to Paris.

The Sunday morning session starts with yours truly expostulating on "The Play of Words"—homographs, homophones, double-sound puns, oxymora, contronyms, and spoonerisms. The verbivorous weekenders should by this time be whacked out on words, but the audience has not lost any of its enthusiasm, and the lecture room is packed. Even those who must leave before lunch are in attendance, holding coats and hand luggage. It is gratifying to see that their joie de lex is not at all dimmed by the promises they have to keep to the outside world.

At the end of my talk, Faire Hart, Mohonk's director of public relations, slips a note into my hand. Her dancing homophones and double-sound puns show that this fair heart, with her homophonous name, has thoroughly imbibed the spirit of my presentation: "Deer Rich heard, Eye deed knot no weather two scent ewe eh Lederer too tank ewe four thee wheeze dumb. Aye dee sided knot two.—Sin Sear Lie, eh Neo Fight"

After so many years of overseeing the Wonderful World of Words weekend, Faire is surely more than a *neophyte*, a down-to-earth word that has grown from two Greek etymons, or word parts, that mean "newly planted." The real neophytes at the wordy weekend have found that they can dig down to the roots of language and draw as much sustenance from words as do the most deeply planted wordophiles.

PLANE TALK

Like Billy Pilgrim in Kurt Vonnegut's *Slaughterhouse Five*, I often become unstuck in time.

While tooting around on a promotional book tour, I suddenly find myself at one o'clock in the morning on a Wednesday, which means that I must have just landed in Los Angeles. I've flown in from Denver, where I did an interview with the *Denver Post* and a signing at a Denver bookstore. That same day I winged my way to Denver from Houston, where I had done some other radio work and book signings. I've flown from New York to Boston to Philadelphia to Washington, D.C., to Atlanta to Milwaukee to Chicago to Houston to Denver, and I'll be winging my way from Los Angeles to San Francisco to Seattle to Vancouver to Winnipeg to Toronto—one day at a time.

Logging so many air miles, I have been frequently exposed to "plane talk," the loopy jargon of the airline industry. Two wrongs don't make a right, but two Wrights did make an airplane about a century before the initial takeoff of the book you're reading. To learn how flighty and fly-by-the-seat-of-the-pants is our English language, take flight with me on a typical tour day:

I wake up in my hotel room for the night, and I take the elevator down to the lobby. I note that the name *elevator* actually describes only half of what the machines do. Something that elevates goes up, so how can an elevator descend?

It does, though, and I get in a shuttle bus that goes back and forth to the airport terminal. Actually, it goes *forth and back,* since you have to go forth before you can go back. And I don't know about you, but that word *terminal* always scares me when it's in an airport.

On the way to the airport, the bus enters rush-hour traffic. Despite the word *hour,* I notice that, in most big cities, rush hour usually lasts more than sixty minutes. The bus gets caught in a big traffic bottleneck. But it's really a *small* traffic bottleneck because the bigger the bottleneck, the more easily the fluid flows through it. Yet you never hear anyone say, "Boy, this morning I got caught in one of the smallest traffic bottlenecks of my life!"

Now that I'm at the (gasp!) terminal, I ask the airline official behind the counter if I am on a nonstop flight. Fortunately, she says that I am not. That's good because I want the flight to stop somewhere. The trouble with nonstop flights is that you never get down.

At any rate, the voice on the public address system announces that it's time to preboard. *Preboard* strikes me as something that people do *before* they board, but I notice that those who are preboarding are actually boarding.

Then it's time for the rest of us to get on the plane. I don't know about you, but I don't get *on* a plane; I get *in* a plane.

As I am about to get in the plane, one of the flight attendants cautions me, "Watch your head." I rotate my cranium in every direction, but I am still unable to watch my head. Trying to watch your head is like trying to bite your teeth.

A little later, the flight attendant assures us that "the aircraft will be in the air momentarily." I know she's thinking that *momentarily* means "in a moment," but I am among the vanishing band of Americans who believe that *momentarily* means "for a moment." The thought of the plane soaring upward "momentarily" does not soothe my soul.

On the flight, I pray that we won't have a near miss. *Near miss*, an expression that has grown up since World War II, logically means a collision. If a mass of metal hurtling through the skies nearly misses another object, I figure it hits it. *Near hit* is the more accurate term, and I hope to avoid one of those, too.

Then comes the most chilling moment of all. The dulcet voice on the airplane intercom announces that we should fasten our seat belts and secure our carry-on bags because we are beginning our "final descent." *Final descent!* Hoo boy, does that sound ominous. I pray that we passengers will live to experience other descents in our lives. No wonder that some people experience fear of flying. What they really feel is fear of crashing!

Incredibly, the aircraft touches down with all of us alive and begins to taxi on the runway. If planes taxi on runways, I wonder, do taxis plane on streets? Now the same voice asks us to keep our seat belts fastened until the aircraft "comes to a complete stop." That reassures me, as I wouldn't want the vehicle to come to "a partial stop," which, of course, would be an oxymoron.

Finally, the vehicle does come to a complete stop, and we are told that we can safely deplane. After that, I'll decab, decar, or debus and enter another hotel. The next morning I'll wake up to face another day of plane talk.

RADIO DAYS

I love radio people," says Richard Lederer ex-statically. In the hundreds of in-studio and on-the-telephone interviews that I have done with radio broadcasters around the United States and the United Kingdom, I have discovered that the English language is in good mouths with radio people. Almost all the radio folk who have interviewed me have actually read the book we're supposed to be talking about and have been genuinely excited about the material. I have been delighted, but not surprised; words are the stuff that radio is made on, and radio broadcasters earn their livings painting pictures with words.

Thanks to the magic of teleconferencing, often the format for a given show is call-in, and the phones and airwaves crackle with logolepsy. I truly get my audio radiance from my radio audience. When people ask me if I miss teaching, my happy experiences on the radio lead me to answer, "I haven't left teaching." In a less intimate but broader way, I now reach more people in a month than in a lifetime of teaching, especially through my regular shows on San Diego, Wisconsin, Rochester, San Francisco, Toronto, and Boston public and commercial radio.

At times, the teacher becomes the student, and I learn something new from the callers. Once on *New York and Company*, the popular New York public radio call-in show hosted by Leonard Lopate, a listener called wanting to know my opinion of the origin of the phrase *the spitting image*. I offered two possible explanations: One theory maintains that *the spitting image* is derived from "the spirit and image" (the inner and outer likeness) and that in Renaissance English and southern American speech *spirit* became *spi'it*, with the *r* dropped. A second hypothesis proposes that *spitting* really means what it says and that *the spitting image* carries the notion of the offspring's being "identical even down to the spit" of the parent.

Immediately the WNYC studio switchboard lit up with listeners eager to expound their theories. Quoting idioms from various languages, callers demonstrated that the metaphor is truly salivary. In French, for example, the expression is *C'est son père tout craché*. ("He is his father all spat out.") Great expectorations! For the first time I could be certain that the second explanation of *the spitting image* was the correct one.

While I was doing a show via telephone with host Davis Rankin on KURV, a small station in southwest Texas, a listener called to ask about the origin of the word *malarkey*. I responded that I had consulted many reputable dictionaries about this word, and all had sighed, "origin unknown." A few minutes later a caller named Lynn got on the line to disagree. She claimed that she was descended from an Irish family named Malarkey, in which the men were reputed for their great size and athletic feats. As tall Irish tales about the Malarkeys' prowess spread, *malarkey* came to be a synonym for *blarney*, another word of Irish descent, originating with the Blarney stone, at Blarney Castle, near Cork. Those who are courageous enough to hang by their heels and kiss the stone are rewarded with the gift of persuasive gab.

Who knows? Lynn's explanation could be a bunch of malarkey, or she could know whereof she speaks. If she is right, she has enriched our knowledge of the origins and development of a beguiling English word.

One of my favorite forums for interviews and call-ins is *The Jim Bohannon Show*, on which I've had the great pleasure of appearing several times. Jim is the exuberant and highly verbivorous host of the three-hour talk show that airs from Arlington, Virginia. *The Jim Bohannon Show* is on a clear channel that reaches almost every state in the U.S.A., and when Jim opens the lines for callers, the in-studio telephone board incandesces. From Maine to California, from Florida to Washington State, one can hear the multifold accents and concerns that reflect a sprawling and diverse nation of speakers. Best of all, Jim doesn't just interview me; he himself enters into the spirit of the wordplay. Here, just about verbatim and with a minimum of cutting and polishing, is a swatch of call-ins and responses that illustrate just how lively and well is the state of the English language in our states. Jim's opening interview with me has just ended, and we go to the call-in segment of the show:

JB: All right, your turn. Let's go to the phones right now. The number is 703-685-2177. Hello, Portland, Oregon.

Caller: Hi. Why does no word rhyme with *orange*?

RL: It's not true that no word rhymes with *orange*. You see, Jim, there are a number of words that are famous for being unrhymable, and the two most famous are *orange* and *silver*. However, there was a man—I'm not kidding—named Henry Honeychurch Gorringe. He was a naval commander who, in the mid-nineteenth century, oversaw the transport of Cleopatra's Needle to New York's Central Park. Pouncing on this event, the poet Arthur Guiterman wrote:

> *In Sparkhill buried lies a man of mark*
> *Who brought the Obelisk to Central Park,*
> *Redoubtable Commander H. H. Gorringe,*
> *Whose name supplies the long-sought rhyme for* orange.

Or you can bend the rules of line breaks and sound as Willard Espy did:

> *Four eng-*
> *ineers*
> *Wear orange*
> *brassieres.*

So *orange* is rhymable.

Caller: And I have a pun for you: Why is Daffy Duck so daffy? Because he smokes quack.

RL: Very good. Now, I've got a duck pun for you. Who was the only duck president of the United States, sir?

Caller: Abraham Lincoln?

RL: Pretty close. Mallard Fillmore. You can't duck that one.

JB: And there was the great duck explorer—Francis Drake. . . . Philadelphia, you're on the air.

Caller: What is a thirteen-letter word in which the first eight letters mean "the largest," and the complete word means "the smallest"?

RL: Oh boy, you've got me.

JB: Oh, I know—*infinitesimal*.

Caller: Correct. You're too good, Jim.

JB: Kansas City is next as we talk with Richard Lederer.

Caller: There was a little country that was chastised by all the other countries because it was a bad little country. The other countries wouldn't throw any commerce the little country's way, so it kept yelling, "O grab me! O grab me!" Well, all the other countries thought that turning the tables was fair play, so here's what they did: "Embargo."

RL: That's a very clever semordnilap, a palindrome that reads backwards. *Embargo* is "O grab me" reversed.

JB: Nashua, New Hampshire, you're on the air.

RL: Woooo, Nashua, one of *my* people.

Caller: Yes, a fellow Granite Stater.

RL: We take nothing for granite there. Go ahead.

Caller: What's the deal between "I could care less" and "I couldn't care less"?

RL: The deal is that logically you couldn't care less. If you say that you could care less, then you care to some extent and are being careless about "care less." But remember, sir, that negatives are very unstable in English, so we say, "Let's see if we can't do it" when we mean, "Let's see if we can do it." Or "I really miss not seeing you" really means, "I really miss seeing you."

JB: We go to Houston next, hello.

Caller: I'm a big fan of puns. We use them a lot at work. They're good for cutting the seriousness away from things. One of the little things we do at work. We take a phrase like "the leading edge of technology," and we say, "Bakers are on the kneading edge of technology," "Taxicab drivers are on the fleeting edge of technology," and "Lawyers are on the pleading edge of technology."

JB: And doctors are on the bleeding edge of technology.

RL: Stockbrokers are on the greeding edge of technology.

Caller: And gardeners are on the weeding edge.

RL: Or on the seeding edge.

JB: And very shortly after this show we're going to have an announcer on the reading edge. He's going to update us on the news. Sault Sainte Marie, Canada, you're next with Richard Lederer.

Caller: I just wanted to ask Richard a couple of spelling words. What do the letters M-A-C-D-U-F-F spell?

RL: Macduff.

Caller: And what does M-A-C-I-N-T-O-S-H spell?

RL: Macintosh.

Caller: And what does M-A-C-H-I-N-E-R-Y spell?

RL: I don't want to ruin your night, ma'am, but it's *machinery*, not *MacHinery*.

JB: We go to Hamden, Connecticut.

Caller: Heaveno, Jim; heaveno, Richard.

JB: This is a man who does not like to say "hello" because this is a family program. He prefers to say, "heaveno."

Caller: There are three groups of words: *sun* and *fun*, which are similar; *woo* and *wound*, which are opposites; and *toast* and *coast*, which are unrelated. It seems that in a good language, words that sound the same should mean the same.

RL: I beg to differ. Language reflects the fearful asymmetry of the human race, and you can't get that kind of logic. In a perfectly logical language, if *pro* and *con* are opposites, then is *congress* the opposite of *progress*? I mean we have a language in which "what's going on?" and "what's coming off?" mean the same thing, while a wise man and a wise guy are opposites, a language in which the third hand on a clock or watch is called the second hand and your nose can run and your feet smell. I'm not looking for logic in language, because human beings, not computers, make language, and we're not logical.

JB: Indianapolis, you're on the air with *The Jim Bohannon Show.*

Caller: Why did they use to name hurricanes with female names? Because otherwise they'd have been him-icanes. The reason I called is—I thought you'd get a kick out of this—I can't see, and every once in a while I meet a young lady that I'd like to get acquainted with, and my favorite line is, "Would you like a blind date?"

RL: Very funny. You are sightless, sir?

Caller: Yes, I am. And I have run into—oops, there's another figure of speech—some short women. I'm presently dating a girl who's four foot three, and I told her that it's better to have loved a short girl than never to have loved a tall.

RL: Oooooh, this guy is very good. Have you heard about the blind fellow who takes his seeing eye dog into a store and the man picks up the dog and whirls it around over his head. The shopkeeper asks, "What are you doing?" And the blind man says . . .

Caller: "We're just browsing."

JB: This is Baltimore next.

Caller: Mr. Bohannon, I'd like to ask Mr. Lederer a question about words. There are three words in the English language that end in *g-r-y*. Two of them are *angry* and *hungry*. What is the third?

RL: Thank you for asking that, sir. You have given me a wonderful opportunity to perform a great service to the American people because what you are quoting is one of the most outrageous linguistic hoaxes in this country.

The answer is that there is no answer, at least no satisfactory answer. May I advise anybody who happens on the *angry* + *hungry* + ? poser, which slithered onto the American scene around 1975, to stop wasting time and to move on to a more productive activity, like counting the number of angels on the head of a pin or searching for a way to write the sentence "There are three *twos* (*to's*, *too's*) in the English language."

There are at least fifty -*gry* words in addition to *angry* and *hungry*, and every one of them is either a variant spelling, as in *augry* for *augury*, *begry* for *beggary*, and *bewgry* for *buggery*, or ridiculously obscure, as in *anhungry*, an obsolete synonym for *hungry*; *aggry*, a kind of variegated glass bead much in use in the Gold Coast of West Africa; *puggry*, a Hindu scarf wrapped around the helmet or hat and trailing down the back to keep the hot sun off one's neck; or *gry*, a medieval unit of measurement equaling one-tenth of a line.

A much better puzzle of this type is, "Name a common word, besides *tremendous*, *stupendous*, and *horrendous*, that ends in -*dous*." Why don't we invite the callers to submit their opinions on this one?

JB: West Palm Beach, Florida, you're next.

Caller: Yes, Mr. Lederer, does a person graduate college or graduate from college?

RL: Or is the person graduated from college? Logically, one is graduated from college since the college confers the degree on the students. That has changed, and educated people are perfectly comfortable with the active-voice "graduate from college." I'd avoid "graduate college." It's awkward and sounds as if the person is doing the graduating of the institution.

JB: Athens, Georgia, you're on the air.

Caller: I have a pun for Mr. Lederer. A member of a New York State family had committed a murder and been electrocuted at Sing-Sing. To put the best face on the affair, this man's descendants would say that the man once occupied the Chair of Applied Electricity in one of the state's leading institutions.

RL: A wonderful example of a euphemism, calling a spade a heart.

JB: Gaithersburg, Maryland, you're on the air.

Caller: I want to share a true pun opportunity that came up many years ago. I was coordinating a serious business meeting, the attendance of which was supposed to include a gentleman named Cappella, and at the last minute we got a note that Mr. Cappella was unable to attend the meeting. I remarked that the meeting would have to be held a Cappella—and got nothing but cold stares.

RL: Your colleagues are just jealous. As Oscar Levant once said, "A pun is the lowest form of humor, when you don't think of it first."

JB: This is Clackamas, Oregon.

Caller: I've got one thing to ask. I used to tell quite a lot of puns myself, until I learned that there was some danger to it, so I gave them up. My main fear in the afterlife was eternal punnish-ment.

JB: We go to Austin, Texas. Richard Lederer is on with you. Hello.

Caller: Good evening. Did you ever get an answer for the fourth word ending in *-dous?*

JB: No, and thanks for reminding us. OK, *tremendous, stupendous, horrendous*—and . . .

Caller: *Hazardous.**

---

*At least thirty-two additional *-dous* words repose in various dictionaries: *antropodous, apodous, blizzardous, cogitabundous, decapodous, frondous, gastropodous, heteropodous, hybridous, iodous, isopodous, jeopardous, lagopodous, lignipodous, molybdous, mucidous, multifidous, nefandous, nodous, octapodous, palladous, paludous, pudendous, repandous, rhodous, sauropodous, staganopodous, tetrapodous, thamphipodous, tylopodous, vanadous,* and *voudous.*

THE COLLIDE-O-SCOPE

OF LANGUAGE

HOW WISE IS

PROVERBIAL WISDOM?

A proverb is a well-known, venerable saying rooted in philosophical or religious wisdom. Just about everybody knows some proverbs, and we often base decisions on these instructive maxims. But when you line up proverbs that spout conflicting advice, you have to wonder if these beloved aphorisms aren't simply personal observations masquerading as universal truths:

How can it be true that you should look before you leap, but make hay while the sun shines? It's better to be safe than sorry, but nothing ventured, nothing gained. Haste makes waste, but he who hesitates is lost. Patience is a virtue, but opportunity knocks but once. Slow and steady wins the race, but gather ye rosebuds while ye may. A stitch in time saves nine, but better late than never. Don't count your chickens before they're hatched, but forewarned is forearmed. Never put off till tomorrow what you can do today, but don't cross that bridge until you come to it. There's no time like the present, but well begun is half done. All things come to him who waits, but strike while the iron is hot. Fools rush in where angels fear to tread, but faint heart never won fair maiden.

We often proclaim that actions speak louder than words, but at the same time we contend that the pen is mightier than the sword.

Beware of Greeks bearing gifts, but don't look a gift horse in the mouth.

There's no place like home and home is where the heart is, but the grass is always greener on the other side and a rolling stone gathers no moss.

A penny saved is a penny earned, but penny wise and pound foolish.

The best things in life are free, but you get what you pay for.

Where ignorance is bliss, 'tis folly to be wise because what you don't know can't hurt you, but it is better to light one candle than to curse the darkness because the unexamined life is not worth living.

Too many cooks spoil the broth and two's company, but three's a crowd. On the other hand, many hands make light work, and two heads are better than one because the more the merrier.

If at first you don't succeed, try try again, but don't beat a dead horse.

Fortune favors the brave, but discretion is the better part of valor.

Silence is golden, talk is cheap, and actions speak louder than words, but the squeaky wheel gets the grease and a word to the wise is sufficient.

Clothes make the man because seeing is believing, but beauty is only skin deep because appearances are deceiving, you can't judge a book by its cover, still waters run deep, and all that glitters is not gold.

Early to bed, early to rise makes a man healthy, wealthy, and wise, but all work and no play makes Jack a dull boy because idle hands are the devil's workshop.

Birds of a feather flock together, but opposites attract. Blood is thicker than water, but familiarity breeds contempt.

Boys will be boys, but spare the rod and spoil the child and children should be seen but not heard.

Variety is the spice of life, but don't change horses in midstream.

The road to hell is paved with good intentions, but it's the thoughts that counts.

There is nothing permanent except change and you never step in the same river twice, but there is nothing new under the sun and the more things change, the more they stay the same.

You can't teach an old dog new tricks and there's no fool like an old fool, but live and learn. Out of the mouths of babes and sucklings comes wisdom, but with age comes wisdom.

The bigger, the better, but the best things come in small packages.

Absence makes the heart grow fonder, but out of sight, out of mind.

What will be will be, but life is what you make it.

When it rains, it pours, but lightning never strikes twice in the same place.

Don't bite off more than you can chew, but hitch your wagon to a star.

What's sauce for the goose is sauce for the gander, but one man's meat is another man's poison.

Might makes right and only the strong survive, but a soft answer turns away wrath and the meek shall inherit the earth.

Turn the other cheek, let bygones be bygones, and forgive and forget, but an eye for an eye and a tooth for a tooth because revenge is sweet and turnabout is fair play.

Share and share alike, but possession is nine-tenths of the law.

A rolling stone gathers no moss, but don't burn your bridges behind you.

Faith will move mountains, but if the mountain won't come to Muhammad, Muhammad must go to the mountain.

Do unto others as you would have them do unto you, but all's fair in love and war.

Virtue is its own reward, but only the good die young.

Two wrongs don't make a right, but the ends justify the means.

It's not whether you win or lose but how you play the game and winning isn't everything, but to the victor goes the spoils.

So for better days ahead, all you have to do is figure out which proverb to use under which circumstances! Quite apparently, whichever side of an argument one takes, one can usually find a proverb to support it. That's why Miguel Cervantes wrote, "There is no proverb that is not true," while Lady Montagu proclaimed that "general notions are generally wrong."

WORDS THAT NEVER STRAY

W hat do the following dozen words have in common: *galore, extraordinaire, akimbo, aplenty, aweigh, incarnate, fatale, royale, par excellence, immemorial, aforethought,* and *manqué?* The answer is that the dozen are "deferential words." While the vast majority of adjectives usually precede the nouns they modify, the words in this list always come after the noun they modify.

What do these words have in common: *bread, clams, dough, cabbage, lettuce,* and *chicken feed?* Each is a food that is metaphoric slang for "cash."

What characteristic do the following words share: *any, beady, cagey, cutie, decay, easy, empty, envy, essay, excel, excess, icy, ivy, kewpie, seedy,* and *teepee?* Each word is cobbled from the sounds of two letters—*NE, BD, KG, QT, DK, EZ, MT, NV, SA, XL, XS, IC, IV, QP, CD, TP.*

None of these clusters approaches the fascination of another group of words that I have been tracking for a decade. Read on, O fellow verbivore, and I trust that the category will gradually come into focus.

Hoping to make some clean lucre, I'm going to get a discussion in edgewise about a special category of words. Unless I give this topic long shrift, I'll be in rotten fettle and guilty of immoral turpitude. Please don't hurl aspersions at these words. I'd prefer that your dander and hackles be down and that you wait on tenterhooks with bated curiosity.

The above paragraph was pretty weird, wasn't it? In fact, it was anything but in kilter. That's because lucre can never be clean, only filthy, and only a word can be gotten in edgewise. Although some people are given a lot of time to shrive (confess), we can speak about shrift only as being short. Fettle must be fine, turpitude must be moral, and aspersions can only be cast—never hurled, spoken, or written. Dander can only be gotten up and hackles raised. Nothing can ever be *off* tenterhooks, and bated can modify only breath.

What is so odd about words such as *lucre, edgewise, shrift, fettle, turpitude, aspersions, dander, hackles, tenterhooks, bated,* and *kilter?* Their commonality is that they are always yoked to one—and only one—other word or phrase.

My friend Al Gregory is a New York postman who lets neither snow, nor rain, nor heat, nor gloom of night stay him from delivering a clever idea in language. Al calls these "monogamous words" because they are always married to one specific word or phrase, and those marriages have withstood the ravages of time. Linguist and lexicographer David Grambs labels these idiosyncratic words "special-team players, not all-round or all-game players." Marshaling another analogy, Grambs writes, "Such words are today virtually one-idiom-only words, having almost no life in the English language beyond the discrete phrase they've become a part of, like fossilized insects preserved in amber."

Many of these single-idiom words have fascinating origins:

Shrift is the noun form of *shrive,* "to confess before a priest." The compound "short shrift" originally referred to the brief time that a condemned prisoner had to make a confession and receive absolution. *Tenterhooks* are hooks that hold cloth on a tenter, a framework for stretching cloth. *To be on tenterhooks* is to be in a state of great tension or suspense. *Bated* is a shortened form of *abated.* That's why *waiting with bated breath* means "waiting with breath held back."

Let's make a game of it. Here are more than a hundred (!) additional examples of monogamous, special-team words. Fill in each blank with the one and only word or phrase that completes each idiom. Only after you've tried your best may you turn to "Answers to Games and Quizzes" on pages 285–87.

1. _____ amok; 2. _____ askance; 3. _____ umbrage; 4. bide _____ _____; 5. _____ sanctum; 6. _____ akimbo; 7. _____ _____auspices _____; 8. ulterior _____; 9. _____ aback; 10. _____ aforethought.

11. _____ _____ tizzy; 12. _____ haywire; 13. _____ pickings; 14. _____ cahoots; 15. _____ _____ immemorial; 16. _____ bumpkin; 17. _____ geezer; 18. _____ wroth; 19. _____ throes _____; 20. _____ loggerheads.

21. _____ _____ trice; 22. _____ _____ druthers; 23. _____ riddance; 24. _____ dint _____; 25. _____ _____ offing;

26. _____ _____ behest; 27. _____ _____ nother; 28. _____ _____ lam; 29. _____ _____ nothings; 30. _____ _____ breather.

31. _____ muckamuck; 32. vantage _____; 33. _____ unawares; 34. misspent _____; 35. _____ trove; 36. wishful _____; 37. gainful _____; 38. barefaced _____; 39. wend _____ _____; 40. wreak _____.

41. unsung _____; 42. foregone _____; 43. scot-_____; 44. briny _____; 45. lickety-_____; 46. busman's _____; 47. _____ roughshod; 48. breakneck _____; 49. blithering _____; 50. sleight _____ _____.

51. _____ _____ kibosh _____; 52. _____ klatch; 53. _____ bended _____; 54. _____ dudgeon; 55. _____ arrears; 56. chock-_____; 57. dipsy _____; 58. Pyrrhic _____; 59. _____ _____ _____ wont; 60. workaday _____.

61. _____ bygones _____ _____; 62. _____ _____ that-away; 63. _____ _____ shebang; 64. fatted _____; 65. graven _____; 66. artesian _____; 67. pinking _____; 68. suborn _____; 69. _____ suasion; 70. scruff _____ _____ _____.

71. _____ aweigh; 72. _____-duper; 73. nitty-_____; 74. _____tock; 75. _____ reflux; 76. raring _____ _____; 77. _____ dragout; 78. gibbous _____; 79. _____ _____ yore; 80. circadian _____.

81. _____-fledged; 82. swaddling _____; 83. self-fulfilling _____; 84. _____ _____ nth _____; 85. _____-aggrandizement; 86. _____ _____ middling; 87. macular _____; 88. _____ apnea; 89. neap _____; 90. _____ unquote.

Now try some pairs connected by *and*:

91. beck _____ _____; 92. spick _____ _____; 93. null _____ _____ _____; 94. vim _____ _____; 95. kith _____ _____; 96. betwixt _____ _____; 97. _____ _____ tucker; 98. _____ haw; 99. _____ _____ wherefores; 100. _____ _____ yon; 101. _____ _____ thither; 102. _____ _____ caboodle; 103. _____ _____ fro; 104. _____ _____ abet; 105. _____ _____ alack.

THE LONG AND THE SHORT OF IT

We human beings are fascinated with the largest and smallest of all manner of things—giants and dwarfs, the most colossal and minature animals, the tallest and lowest trees. Wordaholics! Logolepts! Verbivores of all ages! Step right up to an exhibit of some of the most fascinating specimens of all—the longest and shortest words!

Longest word in standard English dictionaries: *pneumonoultramicroscopicsilicovolcanoconiosis*, a forty-five-letter word for black lung disease.

Longest words in common use: *counterrevolutionaries* and *deinstitutionalization*, both twenty-two letters.

Longest one-syllable-word: *squirreled.*

Longest word with a single vowel: *strengths.*

Longest isogram, a word in which no letter is repeated: *uncopyrightable*.

Longest grammagram, a word consisting entirely of letter sounds: *expediency*, which can be represented as *XPDNC*.

Longest homophonic anagram, that is, two words that are spelled differently but that sound alike and that contain the same letters: *discrete*, *discreet*.

Longest heteronyms, two words that are spelled the same but are pronounced differently: *unionized* (the presence of labor unions) and *unionized* (not ionized).

Longest capitonym, a capitalized word that changes pronunciation when lowercased: *Breathed* (cartoonist Berkeley Breathed, of "Outland") and *breathed*.

Longest anagrammable words: *conversationalists*, *conservationalists*.

Longest common palindromic word, one that can be read forward and backward: *redivider*.

Longest uncommon palindromic word: *kinnikkinnik*, a mixture of sumac leaves, dogwood bark, and bearberry smoked by the Cree Nation in the Ohio valley.

Longest palindromic word in another language: *saippuakivikauppias*, a nineteen-letter Finnish word designating a soap or lye dealer.

Longest words that are reverse images of each other: *stressed—desserts*.

Longest univocalic word, one that contains a single vowel repeated: *strengthlessness*.

Longest snowball word, composed of words that increase one letter at a time: *temperamentally*, which can be divided into *t em per amen tally*.

Longest reverse snowball word: *plainclothesmen*, which can be divided into *plain clot he's me n*.

Longest kangaroo word: Inside *rambunctious* appear, in order, the letters in the smaller synonym *raucous*.

Longest word with the most letters in alphabetical place: In *archetypical*, the letters *a, c, e, i,* and *l* each appear in their natural slots in the alphabet.

Longest word that can be beheaded: Remove the first letter of *presidentially* and you are left with *residentially*.

Longest word that can be curtailed: Remove the last letter of the word *bulleting* and you are left with *bulletin*.

Longest words that can integrate all five major vowels: *blander, blender, blinder, blonder, blunder; patting, petting, pitting, potting, putting*.

Longest word lacking a major vowel: *rhythms*.

Longest words that can be typed on a single row of a type-writer: *peppertree, proprietor, repertoire,* and—ta dah!—*type-writer.*

Longest transposals of the two halves of a word: *kingpin—pinking; raining—ingrain.*

Shortest word in which all five major vowels appear: *sequoia.*

Shortest common word with *aeiou* in order: *facetious.*

Shortest uncommon word with *aeiou* in order: *caesious,* a bluish or gray-green color.

Shortest word with *aeiou* in reverse order: *unnoticeably.*

Shortest word without a vowel: *nth.*

Shortest word in which one letter appears five times: *assesses.*

Shortest heteronym: *do.*

Shortest capitonyms: *Guy* and *Job.*

Shortest readable pangram, a statement that uses the twenty-six letters of the alphabet: "Mr. Jock, TV quiz Ph.D., bags few lynx."

Shortest verse in the Bible: "Jesus wept." (John 11:35)

Shortest poems:

On the Antiquity of Microbes

> *Adam*
> *Had 'em.*

On the Questionable Importance of the Individual

> *I . . .*
> *Why?*

Shortest correspondence: In 1862, the French author Victor Hugo was on holiday. Eager to know how his new novel, *Les Miserables*, was selling, Hugo wrote his New York publisher: "?" Came the reply: "!"

Shortest statement: "I am." (Only three letters.)

Longest sentence (pun alert!): "I do."

OUR UPPITY ENGLISH LANGUAGE

It's time to catch up on *up*, the ever-present two-letter word that may have more meanings than any other and, at times, no meaning at all. It's easy to understand *up* when it means skyward or toward the top of a list. And clearly there are crucial differences between *call* and *call up* and *beat* and *beat up*. But I have to wonder why we warm ourselves up, why we speak up, why we shower up, why a topic comes up, and why we crack up at a joke.

Let's face up to it: We're all mixed up about *up*. Usually the little word is totally unnecessary. Why do we light up a cigar, lock up the house, polish up the silverware, and fix up the car when we can more easily and concisely light, lock, polish, and fix them?

At times, verbs with *up* attached mess up our heads and screw up our minds with bewildering versatility. To look up a chimney means one thing, to look up a friend another, to look up a word something else. We can make up a bed, a story, a test, our face, and our mind, and each usage has a completely different meaning.

At other times, *up-* verbs are unabashedly ambiguous. When we wind up our watch, we start it; when we wind up a meeting, we stop it. When we hold up our partners on the tennis court, are we supporting or hindering them? How, pray tell, can we walk up and down the aisle at the same time and slow up and slow down at the same time?

What bollixes up our language worse than anything else is that *up* can be downright misleading. A house doesn't really burn up; it burns down. We don't really throw up; we throw out and down. We don't pull up a chair; we pull it along. Most of us don't add up a column of figures; we add them down.

And why is it that we first chop down a tree, and then we chop it up?

Maybe it's time to give up on the uppity *up*.

REAL-LIFE LINGUISTICS

Many people picture linguists, those who study language scientifically, as gray-bearded professors with their egg-heads in the clouds, their bespectacled eyes fastened to the pages of ponderous, dusty dictionaries, and their feet firmly planted on midair. In reality, there are occasions when linguists are very much involved in reality and can apply their knowledge of language to real-life legal and business situations. I know because I am occasionally called upon to help name products and devise slogans, and I have testified as an expert witness in a number of court cases that wheeled on the wording of a contractual clause or statute.

In 1987, more than forty-six thousand Maine citizens signed a petition calling for a July 4, 1988, halt to operations at the Maine Yankee Nuclear Power Plant. Traditionally, such petitions are sent to the state legislature and are then submitted to a statewide vote in the form of ballot referenda. Hoping that the legislature would consider rewording the choice before it reached the voters, the management of Maine Yankee hired me as a consulting linguist to analyze the wording of the question that was to appear on the fall ballot:

DO YOU WANT TO LET ANY POWER PLANT
LIKE MAINE YANKEE
OPERATE AFTER JULY 4, 1988,
IF IT MAKES HIGH LEVEL NUCLEAR WASTE?

Whatever my personal and political views regarding nuclear power plants, I felt that as a caring linguist I could apply my skills and experience to help ensure that the question adhered to Maine law mandating that all such referenda be cast in "clear, concise, and direct language." After a great deal of analysis, I concluded and reported that the wording, especially the sections "like Maine Yankee" and "if it makes high level nuclear waste," was ambiguous and the format nontraditional. Here is the gist of my report, the analysis of a professional language scientist:

My handy desk dictionary defines *like*, when used as a preposition, as "having the characteristics of; similar to." In the minds of most people the difference between the phrases "power plants *like* Maine Yankee" and "power plants, *such as* Maine Yankee" is that the first excludes Maine Yankee from the targeted plants and considers only plants with similar characteristics, while the second cites Maine Yankee as one of the group.

This misleading use of the preposition *like* creates two related kinds of confusion: First, if "any power plant" is meant to refer to and include Maine Yankee—as those words are indeed meant to—we are stuck with the rhetorical absurdity of saying that Maine Yankee is like Maine Yankee.

Second, it follows that the words "any power plant like Maine Yankee" will imply to most voters that the plant or plants in question are ones similar to, but do not include, Maine Yankee.

To visualize this analysis in concrete, dramatic terms, imagine this scenario: A voter is in favor of keeping the Maine Yankee plant in operation, but that voter does not wish to see additional power plants, plants "like Maine Yankee," built and operating in Maine. This voter could very likely vote "No" in response to the proposed statement because he or she would assume that a "No" vote would stand against the operation of future plants *like* Maine Yankee, but not Maine Yankee itself.

Let's move on to a second flaw in the sentence. We live in an age of great American overspeak in which we are bombarded by repetitive redundancies, such as "free gifts"—even "complimentary free gifts"—and sprays that "kill bugs dead." But all gifts are free by definition, and killing always renders something dead. The ancient Greeks named this kind of rhetorical overkill *pleonasmas*, and the conditional adverb clause in the referendum sentence, "if it makes high level nuclear waste," is a striking example of a pleonasm because nuclear power plants are plants that by definition produce "high level nuclear waste."

Consider this example: If a parent is asked, "Do you want your child to eat eggs that contain cholesterol?" the parent will very likely be led to the conclusion that there exist, or could exist, eggs that are cholesterol-free. But all consumable eggs contain cholesterol, and any parent who responds negatively to the question posed will unknowingly be eliminating eggs from his or her child's diet.

The same is true of the proposed referendum statement.

Rhetoricians universally agree that the words that appear at the end of a given sentence are the most telling because they make the final impression. In the ballot question, the clause "if it makes high level nuclear waste" comes last and conveys the powerful impression that it is possible to eliminate high level nuclear waste from the operation of nuclear power plants.

Thus, a typical voter might reason: "I want Maine Yankee to continue generating power but without producing high level waste. So I'll vote 'No' and force Maine Yankee to stop making those wastes." Like the parent of the egg-eating child, the voter would not realize that he or she would unalterably be shutting down Maine Yankee.

The format of the referendum is equally problematic. It is a time-honored tradition in debating that the issue to be argued in a given debate is always cast so that the affirmative position seeks to change the status quo and the negative position seeks to maintain the status quo: "The death penalty should be abolished throughout the United States," "Under certain conditions mercy killing should be legal."

There are at least two reasons for this traditional casting of debate topics: First, we don't want to waste people's time by proposing status quo questions, such as "The United States should keep operating under the Constitution." Second, because the affirmative seeks to change the status quo, the affirmative traditionally bears the burden of proof. Yet the wording of the ballot question requires that citizens in favor of the status quo—maintaining a nuclear power plant—vote "Yes" and those for change—shutting down Maine Yankee—vote "No." In addition to violating universal debating rules, the illogical formatting of the proposed question runs contrary to the traditions and reverses the intent of Maine's ballot measures.

On May 1, 1987, the *Portland Press Herald* reported that "the Maine Senate capped an emotional debate by refusing to change the wording of the fall ballot." The vote was 19–16. On November 3, 55 percent of Maine voters responded "yes" to the referendum question, allowing the Maine Yankee plant to continue operating.

During my involvement in the Maine Yankee case, I received some agitated mail and telephone calls excoriating me for supporting an environment-destroying nuclear plant. My response was that I simply wished to defend the cause of clear language so that citizens could make informed choices about their sources of power.

Three years after the Maine Yankee litigation, I found myself allied with a very different coalition of concerned citizens. In 1990, Thermo Electron Energy Systems, a Massachusetts-based company, sought permission to build a twenty-eight-megawatt, waste-wood-to-energy $50 million power plant on a forty-one-acre site in the Pelham Industrial Park, located in the northwest corner of Pelham, New Hampshire. In July of 1990, the Pelham Planning Board voted unanimously to accept the project.

Arguing that the facility represented a health hazard to the region, residents of the neighborhoods adjoining the park who opposed the project formed a group called Safe Environment for Southern New Hampshire. Thermo, they contended, would be burning wood and wood byproducts that could contain arsenic, lead, toxic glues, and other pollutants that would have a deleterious impact on the area. A generator operating twenty-four hours a day for seven days a week, wood-chipping machines, and eighteen-wheeler trucks rumbling to and from the site would, they contended, produce another kind of pollution: noise pollution.

The coalition asked me to testify at a special session of the Pelham Zoning Board of Adjustment in March of 1991. The board was convening to review the question of whether or not the Thermo application conformed to the wishes stated in the Pelham zoning statute.

My charge was to interpret the language of that statute, which reads in part: "The following uses shall be permitted in the Industrial District: . . . All light industrial and manufacturing uses." The linguistic question in this case revolved around whether Thermo Electron's wood/energy plant conformed to the town of Pelham's zoning law allowing "light industrial and manufacturing uses."

Attorneys for Thermo Electron argued that the word *light* referred only to *industry* and not to *manufacturing,* that the statute permitted light industry and any level of manufacturing in the zoned area.

As a linguist, I observed in my testimony before the zoning board that to anyone who is a native or experienced speaker of the English language, the adjective *light* in the phrase "All light industrial and manufacturing uses" clearly refers to and modifies both *industrial* and *manufacturing.*

In the pairing "the old man and woman," for example, the assumption of an experienced speaker of English is that the adjective *old* modifies both *man* and *woman.* If the speaker or writer wishes to detach the second noun from the initial adjective, he or she will always provide some cue, as in "the old man and the young woman."

By analogy, I stated that if the framers of the zoning statute had intended *light* to be joined only with *industrial* and not *manufacturing,* they would have modified *manufacturing* with another word, such as *normal* or *heavy,* as in "light industrial and normal manufacturing uses."

I also noted the illogicality of taking the position that *light* modifies only *industrial* and not *manufacturing. The Random House Dictionary of the English Language* (1987) gives as the first meaning of *industry* "the aggregate of manufacturing or technically productive enterprises in a particular field, often named after its principal product: *the automotive industry; the steel industry.*" The third definition is "trade or manufacturing in general."

If *industry* is a specific cluster of manufacturing enterprises, or essentially synonymous with *manufacture,* it makes absolutely no sense to permit only light industry but normal or heavy manufacturing, as the second category would contradict the first. To allow normal or heavy manufacturing but not normal or heavy industry would be an exceedingly strange, even absurd, decision.

In a filed memorandum, attorneys representing Thermo Electron argued that because *industrial* and *manufacturing* were both adjectives defining the word *uses, light* applied only to the first word, *industrial.* In the statement "the light green and brown cloth," where *green* and *brown* are clearly adjectives, *light* modifies *green* but not *brown.* Therefore, in "light industrial and manufacturing use," *light* must modify only *industrial* and not *manufacturing.*

I attempted to rebut this line of reasoning by explaining that "industrial use" and "manufacturing use" were essentially noun expressions, no different from *industry* and *manufacture,* so that *light* is really an adjective. I countered with the example of "a very old and wrinkled man," wherein *very* is also an adverb, yet it clearly modifies both the adjectives *old* and *wrin-*

kled. Even if *light* in the statute is an adverb, it applies to both the adjectives that follow.

It is impossible to assess the impact of my testimony at the Pelham board meeting that night. I can only report that, by a 3–2 vote, the Zoning Board of Adjustment overturned the earlier decision by the Planning Board to accept the plant. After unsuccessful attempts to reinstate its case, Thermo Electron has abandoned its efforts to erect a waste-wood energy plant in the Pelham area.

In 1992, six school systems and students from those systems brought suit against the state of New Hampshire. The petitioners argued that the way the state finances the operation of its public schools violates the New Hampshire Constitution.

The New Hampshire system of school financing relies almost exclusively on local property taxes. These taxes account for more than 90 percent of all revenue for education, direct state participation less than 8 percent, and federal participation less than 3 percent. Nebraska is the next lowest contributor of state funds, providing 24.5 percent of the local cost of education, more than three times the New Hampshire funding level. Property wealth varies considerably among the property-rich and property-poor cities and towns of New Hampshire. As a result of these substantial disparities in property values between school districts, the property tax revenues that may be raised by the districts also vary dramatically.

Petitioners argued that the statutory system does not adequately fund the public schools at a level consistent with Part 2, Article 83, of the New Hampshire Constitution—that the tax structure denies petitioners the equal protection of the law and taxes the citizens of the property-poor towns unreasonably. Here is the article in question:

Knowledge and learning, generally diffused through a community, being essential to the preservation of a free government; and spreading the opportunities and advantages of education through the various parts of the country, being highly conducive to promote this end; it shall be the duty of the legislators and magistrates, in all future periods of this government, to cherish the interest of literature and the sciences. . . .

When a judge threw the case out of Merrimack County Superior Court, plaintiffs' attorneys asked me to review the petition filed in the case and to analyze the wording of Part 2, Article 83, in the state constitution. After examining this material, I agreed to enter the case as an expert witness for the plaintiffs.

My review of the historical context and the language of the constitution presented powerful evidence that the framers were clearly imposing a duty on "legislators and magistrates, in all future periods" to spread educational opportunity throughout New Hampshire in order to preserve the very government that they had just fought the War of Independence to create. The New Hampshire Constitution was written by men who were attempting to form and preserve a government that would keep them free from tyranny and oppression. Therefore, the duties set forth in the constitution were obviously of great significance to the framers, or they would not have enumerated those obligations in such an important document.

When we look at Part 2, Article 83, I argued, we see that this section specifically refers to action that is "essential to the preservation of a free government." *Essential* descends from the Latin *essentia*, the very being of a person or institution (*esse,* "to be"). The sense of "the most important or basic element of anything" is first recorded in English in 1656. A *governor* was in Greek originally a steersman or pilot, and etymologically *government* is designed to steer and pilot the ship of state that carries its citizens. In other words, a government, like a steersman, takes an active role in the direction of the state.

The constitutional fathers recognized that the general diffusion of education (from the Latin *educere,* "to bring out," "to bring up children") throughout the state was crucial to the general diffusion of knowledge and learning throughout the community. The word *duty* comes to us through the Anglo-French, *deute,* "moral or legal obligation." To ensure the achievement of their highest goal of preservation (late Latin, "keep from harm, keep alive") of their democratic vision, the framers placed a duty on "the legislators and magistrates, in all future periods of . . . government, to cherish the interest of literature and the sciences."

Given the historical context, and further considering that the article in question describes what is necessary for the continued "preservation of a free government," we must note the specific use of the word *cherish* in its setting. Here the verb (from French *cher,* "dear") means not only "to hold dear," but also "to treat with fostering care, to foster tenderly, to nurse (children, young creatures)" and "to foster, tend, cultivate (plants)," primary meanings recorded in the *Oxford English Dictionary* and well established by the end of the sixteenth century. This is a verb that requires not only action, but the passing on of something—in this case the opportunities and advantages of education—from the actor (the state) to the receiver (children). As an indication of the importance attached to this cherishing, the framers mandated this duty in perpetuity, "in all future periods of this government."

Part 2, Article 83, is the only place in the entire state constitution where the word *cherish* appears. Recognizing that knowledge and learning were crucial to the perpetuation of their new and free government, the constitutional framers clearly imposed an active duty of protection, an active duty to keep and to guard, an active duty to cultivate and to nurture education in New Hampshire forevermore.

Words are "the skin of living thought," wrote Supreme Court justice Oliver Wendell Holmes Jr. Plaintiffs appealed to the New Hampshire Supreme Court, with my affidavit at the center of their argument, and won. Apparently, my analysis has made a difference in the way New Hampshire pays for its education. After all, laws are acts of language, and language is a subject about which linguists have something to say.

THE HOLY GRAIL OF LETTER PLAY

Even before you begin reading this essay, I can tell you that there's a good chance you're going to say, perhaps before you're even halfway through, that I am a man with too much time on his hands. You'll probably think that I'm drowning in the shallows of language, while I believe that I drink deeply from its depths.

This chapter is the most technical and schematic in the book, and you won't hurt my feelings if you skip it. But if you stick around through this presentation, you will share one of the greatest adventures of my life in language. In the process, you may come to see words as works of art in themselves, as small stages on which the alphabet leaps and pirouettes.

Some words are interesting because they have a unique, spectacular property. *Twenty-nine* is spelled with letters made of straight lines only—twenty-nine of them, to be exact. You can experience the magic of this pleasing coincidence by printing the word while counting each line along the way. *Ambidextrous* ("capable of using both hands with equal ease") is alphabetically ambidextrous. Its left half, *ambide*, uses letters from the left half of the alphabet, and its right half, *xtrous*, uses letters from the right half of the alphabet.

All words, no matter how common or obscure, are interesting, but some are more interesting than others. And out of the some, a few are interesting in more than one way. And out of the few, one word is more fascinating in more ways than any other word in the language. It is packed with properties that range from common to unique. It stands out from the outstanding. What is that word? The quest to find it is the ultimate exercise in wordplay—the search for the Holy Grail of Letter Play.

Over the course of a series of e-missives with Dave Morice—my fellow letter player, the man who discovered the ambidexterity of *ambidextrous*, and the coauthor of this chapter—we noticed something, then many things, about the word *peppertree*, defined in *Merriam-Webster's Collegiate Dictionary, Eleventh Edition*, as "a So. American evergreen tree (*Schinus molle*) of the cashew family grown as a shade tree in mild climates."

Peppertree is a ten-letter pyramid word, a wordplay form that occurs in only a few other words of that length, *sleeveless* and *Tennessee's* being the only others that are fairly common. A pyramid word has one of one letter, two of another, three of a third, and—the outer limits—four of a fourth. For that reason alone, *peppertree* is remarkable.

But then, *peppertree* started revealing itself to be an evergreen of the most alphabetic kind. A second property, related to the first, appeared: *Peppertree* contains two shorter pyramid words, all three of which begin with the first *P* in the host word—possibly a unique case of a pyramid within a pyramid within a pyramid. And then a third property, related to the second, peeked out: Each pyramid after the first is formed by increasing the number of letters in each row by one and by adding a new letter at the top:

PEP	PEPPER	PEPPERTREE
		T
	R	R R
E	E E	E E E
P P	P P P	P P P P

As words go, *peppertree* is neither common nor obscure. It's easy enough to get a general idea of what it means. Including the three pyramids above, there are at least twenty ways in which *peppertree* does something unusual in its letters, pronunciation, and meaning. I believe that it is the Grail word.

• If prefixes are allowed, then *peppertree* is not only a pyramid word but also a snowball word—a one-letter word followed by a two-letter word followed by a three-letter word followed by a four-letter word: *p ep per tree* (*ep* appears in the *Oxford English Dictionary* as a shortened form of *epi*).

• All the letters in *peppertree* can be typed on the *qwerty* row of a typewriter.

• Without its last letter, *peppertre(e)* can be divided into three overlapping palindromes (elements that can be read the same forward and backward)—*pep, eppe,* and *ertre.* They have increasing lengths of three, four, and five letters.

• Without its first letter, *(p)eppertree* can be divided into three palindromes—*eppe, rtr,* and *ee.* They have decreasing lengths of four, three, and two letters.

- Its consonants occur in clusters, each separated by the vowel *e*, that form the most basic arithmetic progression— 1, 2, and 3 (*p, pp, rtr*).

- In uppercase, all the letters in *PEPPERTREE* stand on vertical lines.

- In uppercase, half of its letters have curves, and half don't: *PPPRR* (occurring in alphabetic order); *EETEE* (occurring in palindromic order).

- In uppercase, half of its letters have closed spaces and half don't: *PPPRR, EETEE*.

- In lowercase, each letter in *peppertree* has one line and one curve.

- In lowercase, half of its letters have vertical lines and half have horizontal lines: *ppprr, eetee*.

- In its three syllables, *peppertree* contains three soundings of the letter *e*—short, schwa, and long.

- *Peppertree* is an *evergreen*, and each of these two words is a univocalic using the letter *e* four times.

- Its vowels (*eeee*) are in the first half of the alphabet, and its consonants are in the second half (*ppprtr*).

- Listing each of the four different letters in order of first appearance in *peppertree* spells *pert*, which means "piquantly stimulating," certainly a quality of the dancing alphabet in the word.

- Arranging all the letters of *peppertree* in order of number of occurrences, from greatest to least, results in *eeee ppp rr t*. Alphabetizing all the letters results in the exact same arrangement.

- The letter *P* looks like a leaf. When the *P*'s fall off the *PEPPERTREE*, the remaining letters form a palindrome, *EERTREE*, in which the *T* stands like a tree among the letters that branch out to spell *TREE* in both directions.

- *Peppertree* has two different double-letter strings, *pp* and *ee*. These four letters can be reshuffled to form *peep*, which has several meanings—"a sandpiper (bird)," "a feeble, shrill sound," and "a brief look," to name three. Thus, a baby peep might peep as it peeps out of its nest in the peppertree.

THE ROMANCE OF WORDS

ETYMOLOGICAL SNAPSHOTS

To the man or woman who knows its origin, each word presents a picture, no matter how ordinary it may appear. Sometimes the attrition wrought by time and human memory has ravaged the images so that no trace is left. In other instances, surface grime can be wiped away so that the beauty of the details can be restored and the contours and colors can once again be seen.

For me word pictures are like family snapshots. Discovering the origin of a word or phrase gives me the same pleasure I used to experience when my grandparents, parents, and older brothers and sisters would open up the family album, point to a cluster of sepia photographs, and tell me stories about the people gazing out from the pages. Hearing tales about those who came before me and uncovering those odd, buried, Old World family mysteries helped me learn whence I came and who I am. Words, too, are our forebears. Most were born long before we were, and all bequeath us their rich legacies. Illuminating the faded picture of a time-hallowed word or phrase throws light on our history and our customs, our loving and fighting, our working and playing, our praying and our cursing.

The poet William Cowper once wrote of

> . . . *philologists who trace*
> *A panting syllable through time and space,*
> *Start it at home, and hunt it in the dark*
> *To Gaul, to Greece, and into Noah's ark.*

As an avid word hunter, I love stalking bestial words through time and flushing out the animals that live in the ark of language. Cranberries acquired their name from the Low German *kranbeere*, meaning "crane," because the plant flourishes in marshy lands frequented by cranes. Tiny mice scamper through our bodies because *muscle* derives metaphorically from the Latin *musculus*, diminutive of *mus*, "mouse." A scapegoat was an actual goat upon whose head were symbolically placed all the sins of the ancient Hebrew community. As we read in the Book of Leviticus, the animal was allowed to "escape" into the wilderness, bearing the community's burden of sin and atoning for its transgressions.

If a scapegoat was really a goat, one might wonder, does a dandelion have anything to do with lions? Most certainly. The English used to call the yellow, shaggy weed a "lion's tooth" because the indented ("made jagged, as with a tooth"), pointed leaves resemble the lion's snarly grin. During the early fourteenth century the lion's-tooth plant took on a French flavor and became the *dent-de-lion*, "tooth-of-the-lion." Then it acquired an English accent: *dandelion*.

Toothsome etymologies such as the one for *dandelion* were of great assistance when I was invited to address the members of the New Hampshire Dental Society. A number of dentists will tell you that getting me to sit still in a dentist's chair is like pulling teeth. As a born coward, I am simply unable to transcend dental medication. Still, I was delighted to find out that the oral metaphors in our language provided a topic that I could really "sink my teeth into."

At first I thought that expressions about the teeth would be as scarce as hen's teeth. (Hens, of course, don't have any teeth.) As I began collecting ideas for my talk to the dental society, I believed that I would give my eyeteeth for some good examples.

The eyeteeth, I discovered, are so called because they are located directly below the eyes in the upper jaw, and are called canine teeth because they resemble the pointed teeth of dogs. As such, they are especially useful in holding and tearing food, and they are the most difficult and painful of teeth to extract. Thus, if you would "give your eyeteeth" for something, you are willing to go through a lot to relinquish something of great value.

Teeth are often cited to indicate strength. We talk about an agreement that has teeth in it, being in the teeth of a battle, fighting tooth and nail. We describe strong winds and sarcastic comments as "biting."

Not surprisingly, teeth are also associated with matters culinary. We call some women toothsome, not because they have a lot of teeth, but because their appearance is pleasing to the palate of the eyes. In parts of the country, Italian sandwiches are called *grinders* because it takes a good set of teeth to eat them. Pasta should be cooked *al dente*, "to the tooth"—in other words, cooked just enough to retain a somewhat firm texture for the teeth. Spanish cookbooks call for using a *diente* from a *cabeza* of garlic—that is, a "tooth" from a "head" of garlic.

Teeth are often associated with duplicity. We talk about

people who *lie through their teeth*, that is, who force themselves to assume a calm demeanor that will conceal their true feelings. They display a hearty smile, baring and clenching their teeth as a means of controlling their emotions and pretending that *butter wouldn't melt in their mouths*. Closely related is the expression *to laugh on the wrong side of one's mouth*, which originally meant to laugh in a forced way, perhaps by opening only one corner of the mouth. "Which side of the mouth is the wrong side?" we wonder aloud.

Many phrases from the Book of Job in the Old Testament have become proverbial in our language: "Naked came I from my mother's womb, and naked shall I return"; "The Lord gave, and the Lord hath taken away"; and "My bone cleaveth to my skin, and to my flesh, and I escaped with the skin of my teeth." This last phrase has been altered slightly to *by the skin of my teeth*.

Despite objections that the teeth don't have any skin, centuries of Bible reading have given the expression a permanent place in our language as a description of a close escape. Many interpret the skin in *skin of my teeth* to refer to the enamel covering the teeth, a film as thin as Job's margin of safety.

As with *dandelion*, animals and teeth converge in *mastodon*, the name we assign to those lumbering preelephants. *Mastodon* is cobbled from the Greek *mastos*, "breast" (as in *mastectomy*), and *odont*, "tooth," as in *orthodontia* ("correct teeth"). Mastodons are so named for the nipplelike protuberances on their molars.

The space I've left at the start of each paragraph in this book is an *indentation*. When we indent a paragraph (from the Latin *dens*, "tooth," by way of the French *dent*), we take a chunk, or small bite, out of the beginning. *Indenture*, from the same root, strictly means "a document with serrated edges," referring to the once-common practice of cutting contracts into halves with jagged edges—one half for each party to the agreement. By fitting the edges together, one could authenticate the document.

When we describe a golden ager as *long in the tooth*, we are reflecting on the fact that our gums recede with age, thereby displaying more and more roots. It is the same with horses. The age and health of a horse can be ascertained by examining the condition and number of its teeth. Although an animal may appear young and frisky, a close inspection may reveal that it is *long in the tooth* and ready for the glue factory.

Still, it is considered bad manners to inspect the teeth of a horse that has been given to you and, by extension, to inquire too closely into the cost or value of any gift. Now you know the origin of *don't look a gift horse in the mouth*, one of our oldest proverbs, whinnying back at least fifteen hundred years.

If, on the other hoof, you decide to pay money to a horse trader, you are advised to determine whether it is a young stud or an old nag by examining the teeth and obtaining your information *straight from the horse's mouth*, precisely where responsible word searchers should look.

HAUNTED WORDS

The Greek *etymon* means "true, original," and the Greek ending *-logia* means "science or study." Thus, etymology is supposed to be the science or study of true and original word meanings. But I have learned that the proud house of etymology is populated by all manner of "ghoulies and ghosties and long-leggety beasties" miscreated by spook etymologists. (*Spook* reaches back to the Dutch *spooc*, "ghost, specter.") These sham scholars would rather invent a word origin after the fact than trace it to its true source. Spooks prefer drama and romance to accuracy and truth. With spooks it is sentence first, trial never.

Caveat lexamator: word lover beware. Be wary especially of explanations of labels for food. Eating humble pie has nothing etymologically to do with the word *humble*, "lowly." The dish was really *umble pie*, made from the *umbles*—heart, liver, and other innards—of a deer. The servants and huntsmen had to settle for these innards while the lord of the manor and his guests dined on venison. *Sirloin* is not so called because James I or Henry VIII (according to Thomas Fuller in 1655) or Charles II (according to *The Cook's Oracle* in 1822) knighted his favorite dish, declaring, "Arise, Sir Loin." In truth, *sirloin*, the upper or choicer part of a loin of beef, was borrowed from Middle French *surloigne* (*sur*, "above" + *loigne*, "loin") centuries before any of the monarchs who are credited with honoring the cut of meat. But legends die hard, especially when they are lit by such bright stories, and this particular flight of etymological fancy has survived for more than three centuries as a hoax of wordplay foisted on unsuspecting language lovers.

More culinary spookery has been served up in the game of tennis, where *love* means "no points." The most charming derivation for the use of *love* in this sense is that the word derives from *l'ouef*—"the egg"—because a zero resembles an egg, just as the Americanism "goose egg" stands for "zero." But *un oeuf*, rather than *l'ouef*, would be the more likely French form, and, anyway, the French themselves (and most other Europeans) designate "no score" in tennis by saying "zero." Most tennis historians adhere to a less imaginative but more plausible theory. These more level heads contend that the tennis term is rooted in the Old English expression "neither love nor money," which is more than a thousand years old. Because love is the antithesis of money, it is nothing.

One of the most persistent and spookiest of etymologies is the recurrent wheeze that *posh*, "elegant, swanky," is an acronym for "p(ort) o(ut), s(tarboard) h(ome)," a beguiling bit of linguistic legerdemain that has taken in a company of estimable scholars. When British colonial emissaries and wealthy vacationers made passage to and from India and the Orient, they often traveled along the coast of Africa on the Peninsular and Oriental Steam Navigation Company line. Many of these travelers sought ideal accommodations "away from the weather," on the more comfortable or shady side of the ship. By paying for two staterooms—one portside out, the other starboard home—the very rich could avoid the blazing sun and strong winds both ways, an act of conspicuous consumption that has become synonymous with anything luxurious and ultrasmart.

While the abundant inventiveness here deserves at least a sitting ovation, this etymology of *posh* is, well, bosh. For one thing, neither the travelers' literature of the period nor the records of the famous Peninsular and Oriental Steam Navigation Company show a jot of reference to *posh*. For another, an examination of the deck plans of the ships of the period reveals that the cabins were not placed on the port and starboard sides. For a third, *posh* does not show up in print until 1918. For a fourth, always be suspicious of etymologies that employ acronyms: *cop* does not stand for "constable on patrol" nor *tip*, as a gratuity, for "to insure promptness" nor *news* for "northeast-west-south" nor *golf* for "gentlemen only; ladies forbidden" nor you know what for "for unlawful carnal knowledge."

The editors of the *Oxford English Dictionary* say nothing of any connection with the location of cabins on ships and either ignore or reject outright the acronymic theory, and all reputable dictionaries list the origin as "unknown." Moreover, the monsoon winds that blow in and out of the Asian heartland shift from winter to summer. This fickle phenomenon changes the location of the sheltered and exposed sides of a ship so that in a given season the ideal location can be starboard out, portside home (hence, *soph*). More likely and more mundanely, *posh* hails from a British slang word of the same spelling that means "a dandy," but don't count on it.

About all this I am being completely sincere.

The spooks squeak and gibber that *sincere* issues from the

Latin *sine cera*, the idea being that Roman purveyors of marble and pottery deviously polished their wares with wax to apply a false luster and conceal cracks and holes. Honest merchants, who did not doctor their products, proudly displayed them as being without wax—*sine cera.*

Spook etymologies are haunting your computer in the form of a ubiquitous item titled "Life in the 1500s" that has been dragging its chains around the Internet for years. The color and romance of the word and phrase explanations in the message are as beguiling as can be. One of them is this electronic explanation of a common meteorological phrase: "Houses had thatched roofs. Thick straw, piled high, with no wood underneath. It was the only place for animals to get warm, so all the pets—dogs, cats, mice, rats and bugs—lived in the roof. When it rained it became slippery, and sometimes the animals would slip and fall off the roof. Hence the saying, *It's raining cats and dogs.*"

Dubious. The literal explanation is that during heavy rains in not so Merry Olde England, some city streets became raging rivers of filth, carrying many dead cats and dogs. But there is also strong evidence that the phrase *it's raining cats and dogs* may not be literal. In the Dark Ages, people believed that animals, including cats and dogs, had magical powers. Cats were associated with storms, especially the black cats of witches, while dogs were frequently associated with winds. The Norse storm god Odin was frequently shown surrounded by dogs and wolves. So when a particularly violent storm came along, people would say that *it's raining cats and dogs*, with the cats symbolizing the rain and the dogs representing the wind and storm. This folkloric explanation is supported by such expressions as *it's raining dogs and polecats* and *it's raining pitchforks*.

The e-drivel continues: "Sometimes they could obtain pork and would feel really special when that happened. When company came over, they would bring out some bacon and hang it to show it off. It was a sign of wealth and that a man could really bring *home the bacon*. They would cut off a little to share with guests and would all sit and *chew the fat*."

Ridiculous. Absurd. Here the bacon refers to the greased pig that once figured so prominently in American county fairs. The slippery swine was awarded to whoever caught it, and the winner could take (bring) it home.

Chew the fat is unknown before the American Civil War. One theory contends that sailors working their jaws on the tough salt pork rationed out when supplies ran low constantly grumbled about their poor fare while literally chewing the fat. What seems clear is that "chewing the fat," like "shooting the breeze," provides little sustenance for the amount of mastication involved. Which is just what happens with jerry-built, jury-rigged etymologies.

Now the plot deepens, and our subject turns grave. Some of the most spookily haunted of the explanations in "Life in the 1500s" pertain to death: "Lead cups were used to drink ale or whiskey. The combination would sometimes knock people out for a couple of days. Someone walking along the road would take them for dead and prepare them for burial. They were laid out on the kitchen table for a couple of days and the family would gather around and eat and drink and wait and see if they would wake up. Hence the custom of holding a 'wake.' "

Folderol! Piffle! Poppycock! *Wake* descends from the Middle English *wakien*, "to be awake," and is cognate with the Latin "vigil." *Wake* simply means, traditionally at least, that someone stays awake all night at the side of the casket on the night before the funeral.

Hear ye now the most ghoulish and foolish of the spook etymologies that clank throughout this e-dissertation: "England is old and small, and they started running out of places to bury people. So they would dig up coffins and would take their bones to a house and reuse the grave. In reopening these coffins, one out of twenty-five coffins were found to have scratch marks on the inside, and they realized they had been burying people alive. So they thought they would tie a string on their wrist and lead it through the coffin and up through the ground and tie it to a bell. Someone would have to sit out in the graveyard all night to listen for the bell. Hence the expression *graveyard shift*. They would know that someone was *saved by the bell* or he was *a dead ringer*."

Balderdash! Twaddle! Hooey! Codswollop! Despite high marks for ingenuity, these etymological explanations are merely exercises in free association without regard for attribution. In factories that work around the clock, employees report for work at 8:00 A.M. for the "regular" or "day" shift; at 4:00 P.M. for the "swing" or "night" shift, and at midnight for the "graveyard" shift, lasting until 8:00 A.M. According to Harold Wentworth and Stuart Berg Flexner's *Dictionary of American Slang*, the name *graveyard shift* refers to "the ghostlike hour of employment"—and nothing more.

Dead ringers actually originated at the race track. To take advantage of the long odds against an inferior horse's winning a race, unscrupulous gamblers would substitute a horse of superior ability and similar appearance. Nowadays, *dead ringer* means any close look-alike.

Why *ringer?* Probably because *ringer* was once a slang term for a counterfeiter who represented brass rings for gold ones at county fairs. And *dead* here means "absolute, exact," as in "dead heat" and "you're dead right."

Should I even dignify the windy suspiration about *saved by the bell* with a logical explanation? Oh well, here 'tis, and it's just what you thought in the first place. *Saved by the bell* is nothing more than the obvious—a reference to the bell signaling the end of a round of boxing. No matter what condition a fighter is in during a boxing contest, even if he is being counted out, he is saved by the bell and gains a reprieve once that bell rings.

I do hope that we all gain a reprieve from these idiotic spook etymologies that rattle and clank around the Internet and haunt the halls of our language. That, of course, is the same Internet that knowledgeably informs us that National Public Radio is about to go out of business; that Congress is about to institute an e-mail tax; that a virus is about to crash your computer; that your toilet is about to explode; that antiperspirants, NutraSweet, and canola oil cause just about every malady known to humankind; that Neiman Marcus charges $250 for a chocolate-chip cookie recipe; that a Nigerian businessman will make you rich if you will just make a modest deposit in his account; that 450 years ago Nostradamus predicted the outcome of the 2000 election, the attack on the Twin Towers, and other history-changing events; and that next July we collide with Mars. If you believe everything you glean from cyberspace, especially about language, please get in touch with me. I have a bridge, a lovely parcel of swampland, and a hot dot.com start-up I want to sell you.

MY KIDS THE POKER PLAYERS

My son Howard Lederer and daughter Annie Duke live and move and have their beings in that windowless, clockless pleasure dome known as Las Vegas. I'm pleased to report that they are the only sibling pair ever both to reach the final day of a World Series of Poker event and to have won national tournaments with capacious and impressive names, such as the Diamond Jim Brady Texas Hold'em Shoot-out, the Four Queens Poker Classic in High-Limit Omaha, and the Hall of Fame Classic Deuce-to-Seven Lowball Draw No-Limit. Phew.

My children's achievements in the gaming halls inspire me to deal from a full deck of vivid words and phrases that have made the trip from the poker table into our everyday conversation and writing. The color and high-risk excitement of poker have made the language of the game one of the most pervasive metaphors in our language.

The basic elements of poker are the cards, the chips, and the play of the hand, and each has become embedded in our

167

daily parlance. Beginning with the cards themselves, the verb *to discard* descends from *decard,* "away card," and first meant to reject a card from one's hand. Gradually, the meaning of *discard* has broadened to include rejection beyond cardplaying. A cardsharp who is out to cheat you may be dealing from the bottom of the deck and giving you a fast shuffle, in which case you may get lost in the shuffle. You might call such a low-down skunk *a four-flusher. Flush,* a hand of five cards that are all of one suit, flows from the Latin *fluxus* because all the cards flow together. *Four-flusher* characterizes a poker player who pretends to such good fortune but in fact holds a worthless hand of four same-suit cards and one that doesn't match.

All of these terms originated with poker and other betting card games and have undergone a process that linguists call "broadening." A good example of movement from one specific argot to another is *wild card berth* or *wild card player* as used in football and tennis. In these sports, a team hopes for *back-to-back victories*—from a fortuitous ace-down-ace-up as the first two cards in a game of five-card stud.

Now that I've laid my cards on the table, let's see what happens when the chips are down. Why do we call a gilt-edged, sure-thing stock a *blue-chip stock?* Because poker chips are white, red, and blue, and the blue ones are the most valuable. Why, when we compare the value and power of two things, do we often ask how one *stacks up* against the other, as in "How do the Red Sox stack up against the Yankees?" Here the reference is to the columns of chips piled up before the players around a poker table. These stacks of plastic betting markers also account for the expressions *bottom dollar* and *top dollar. Betting one's bottom dollar* means wagering the entire stack, and the top dollar, or chip, is the one that sits atop the highest pile on the table. Indeed, the metaphor of poker chips is so powerful that one of the euphemisms we use for death is *cashing in one's chips*.

The guts of poker is the betting. *You bet!* has become a standard affirmative in American English, and it is far from being the only betting metaphor that has traveled from the gaming halls to our common vocabulary. If you want to call my bluff on that one and insist that I put up or shut up, I'll be happy to put my money where my mouth is.

Say you're involved in a big business deal. You let the other guy know that you're not a piker running a penny ante operation and that he'd better ante up big. One theory traces *piker*, one who habitually makes small bets, to westward migrants from Pike County, Missouri. These small farmers were less inclined than hardened veterans to risk high stakes, and the county name became eponymously synonymous with penny-pinching cheapness. *Ante*, from the Latin for "before," refers to chips placed in the middle of the poker table before the betting begins, so a penny ante game is fit only for pikers.

The negotiations continue, and you sweeten the pot by upping the stakes. You don't want to blow your wad and go in the hole or in hock, but you don't want to stand pat either. Rather than passing the buck, you play it close to the vest without showing your hand, maintain an inscrutable poker face, keep everything aboveboard, and hope to hit the jackpot.

The hole in the phrase *in the hole* refers to a slot cut in the middle of poker tables through which checks and cash are deposited into a box, to be transferred later to the coffers of the house. *In hock* descends from the game of faro, a cousin of poker. The last card in the box was known as the hocketty card. The player who bet that card was said to be *in hock*, at a disadvantage that could lose him his shirt.

Stand pat comes from the strategy of keeping one's original (pat) hand in draw poker rather than making an exchange. Because card sharps are known to engage in chicanery when their hands are out of sight and under the table, or board, *aboveboard* has come to mean open honesty and *under the table* the opposite. *Playing it close to the vest* ensures that no one else will peek at the contents of a player's hand. *Jackpot* originally described the reward to the big winner in a game of progressive poker, in which you need a pair of jacks or better to "open the pot." Because the stakes grow higher until the requisite pair is dealt, *jackpot* has gradually expanded to include the pots of gold in slot machines, game shows, and state lotteries.

Pass the buck is a common cliché that means "to shift responsibility." But why, you may have asked yourself, should handing someone a dollar bill indicate that responsibility is in any way transferred? Once again the answer can be found in high-stakes gaming halls and riverboats. The *buck* in *pass the buck* was originally a poker term designating a marker that was placed in front of the player whose turn it was to deal the next hand. This was done to vary the order of betting and to keep one person from dealing all the time, thus transferring the disadvantages of being the first to wager and cutting down on the chances of cheating. During the heyday of poker in the nineteenth century, the marker was often a hunting knife whose handle was made of a buck's horn. The marker defined the game as Buckhorn Poker or Buck Poker and gave us the expression *pass the buck*.

In the Old West, silver dollars often replaced buckhorn knives as tokens, and these coins took on the slang name *buck* for their own. Former president Harry S. Truman, reputed to be a skillful poker player, adopted the now-famous motto "The buck stops here," meaning that the ultimate responsibility rested with the president.

The cleverest application of poker terminology that I have ever encountered appears on the truck of a New Hampshire plumbing company: A FLUSH IS BETTER THAN A FULL HOUSE. In poker that isn't true, but a homeowner would recognize its wisdom.

Great poker players must have a firm grounding in the statistics of card distribution and probability. But as my son and daughter, the poker champions, explain: To play poker at the highest level is to read people—their faces, their body language, and their behavior patterns. Language and people are inextricably intertwined. The democratic poetry of poker that pervades our American language is a vivid emblem of the games that we, as a civilization, watch and play.

It's in the cards. You can bet on it.

A MATTER OF
POLITICAL CORRECTNESS

During the call-in segment of my San Diego public radio show, *A Way with Words*, a listener asked me the origin of the expression *Don't take any wooden nickels*. I explained that the meaning of *nickel* as a sum of money entered the American language in 1866, the first year that five-cent pieces containing nickel were minted. During the nineteenth century, commemorative tokens made out of wood were produced as souvenirs. Frequently, such coins were accepted as legal tender while the celebration was in progress, but, of course, they ceased to have value when the bash was over. So *Don't take any wooden nickels* became the popular equivalent of "Watch out that you don't get gypped." Several listeners wrote me to express their "shock" and "disappointment" that I used the word *gyp*, which, they contended, is "a racial slur degrading gypsies." I sincerely appreciate such thoughtful letters, but on the next program I offered a rebuttal:

I fully agree that we must be ever vigilant of perpetrating and perpetuating racial and religious slurs in our speaking and writing. Using *Jew* as a verb is unconscionable, and former president Bill Clinton was rightfully upbraided by a national Welsh group for using *welsh* as a verb to mean "to fail to honor a promise."

The verb *gyp* does turn out to be a clipping of the word *Gypsy* (itself a shorting of *Egyptian*) and hence disparagement of that wandering group. But I feel the word *gyp* has evolved so far beyond the history of Gypsies that we need not banish it from our language. If so, we would have to jettison a host of common words that teem our tongues:

- Two words we use to praise skill are *dexterous*, from the Latin *dexter*, "right," and *adroit*, from the French *à droit*, "to the right." On the other hand (the left one, of course), *sinistra*, Latin for "left hand," yields the pejorative *sinister* in English. The French for "left hand" is *gauche*; in English it means "crude, lacking in social grace." A descendant of *gauche* is *gawky*. Should *sinister*, *gauche*, and *gawky* be banished from the English language?

- The ancients, in their finite wisdom, believed that the womb—or *hyster* in Greek—was an unfixed organ that floated around inside a woman's body, tickling her and making her emotionally unstable or *hysterical*. Hence, *hysteria* is a subtle dig at women, sterotyping them as flighty and emotionally volatile. It was Sigmund Freud who first popularized the notion that men could be hysterical, too.

- *Meretricious* means "attractive in a cheap, gaudy way; alluring by false charms." The adjective derives from the Latin *meretrix*, "prostitute," and insults sex industry workers.

of 8

 88888888888888888888

A Matter of Political Correctness

- The Vandals were members of a Germanic tribe that lived in ancient times and that invaded western Europe in the fourth and fifth centuries A.D. Today a *vandal* denotes a person who acts like a barbarian by willfully destroying beautiful or valuable things.

- *Yankee* may well have begun life as a slur that British colonists hurled at Dutch freebooters in early New York. The Dutch love of cheese was well known, so the British fashioned *Yankee* from the Dutch *Jan Kaas*, which literally meant "John Cheese," combining the Dutch first name *Jan* (pronounced "Yahn") with *Kaas* (the Dutch word for "cheese," the country's national product).

I'm all for political correctness applied in truly caring and careful ways—such as the substitution of *homeless* as an appellation for the bums who used to live on the streets when I was a lad. *Homeless* is a far kinder and more accurate appellation for unfortunate souls who haven't made a choice to be out on the streets. I'm all for terms like *server*, *weatherperson*, and *letter carrier* to avoid unnecessary gender identification in the workplace. I'm proud to be living in a time when a flight attendant can make a pilot pregnant.

But it disturbs me when accusations are thrown around that *red tape* is a slur against Native Americans, that *in a coon's age* demeans African Americans, and that *rule of thumb* is the vestige of a law enjoining a husband from using a stick thicker than his thumb to beat his wife. So imaginative. So bogus. The vast majority of reputable sources indicate that *red tape* descends from the use of reddish tape to tie up official documents, a practice that began in seventeenth-century England.

175

In a coon's age, meaning "in a long time," is built on the erroneous belief that raccoons (or "coons") are long-lived. *Rule of thumb* harks back to days of old, when rulers of the measuring kind were uncommon and people used the length of the thumb from the knuckle to the tip as an approximate measure of one inch—inexact, but better than nothing.

Recently, political correctness ran amok at SUNY Albany. Publicity for an April picnic planned to honor Jackie Robinson for breaking the color barrier in major league baseball was attacked by a student group who wrongly claimed that *picnic* stems from *pickaninny*, a disparaging word for African-American children. The actual derivation is from the seventeenth-century French *picnique*, and has nothing to do with race.

Organizers at the SUNY Albany campus caved in anyway and decided to call the event an "outing." That's when a gay student leader voiced loud objections. In the end, the event was publicized without any title.

Mark Twain quipped that "simplified spelling is all right, but, like chastity, you can carry it too far." It's the same with political correctness. It's all right, but you can carry it too far.

IT'S A PUNDERFUL LIFE

JEST FOR THE PUN OF IT

Once upon a time, the New Hampshire Lawn Tennis Association sponsored a slogan contest. From its beginnings, the organization's letterhead symbol had been two crossed tennis racquets, and the group's president offered a prize, a can of tennis balls, to the member who could serve up the spinniest slogan to go with the logo.

Since I have been an incorrigible (and encourageable) punster all my life, the challenge stirred my blood. As I bounced around a few ideas, I realized what a matchless set-up this contest was. With low overhead, I could drive home my point for a net gain.

Immediately from my childhood I recalled the story of the two cats who were watching a tennis match. One turned to the other and said, "You know, my mother's in that racquet."

I was having a high-strung gut reaction.

Then I had a stroke of good luck. I decided to do some research for my slogan bye reading the world's greatest writers of tennis books. So I opunned the books of Robert W. *Service* and Miguel Cervantes, Lord Byron and Richard Lovelace, Honoré de Balzac and Joseph Addison, and Ivy Compton-Burnett and Kurt Vonnegut. And of course, I read the works of the two greatest authors of all time—Alfred, Lord Tennyson and Tennis E. Williams.

I discovered rich literary gold—*Point Counterpoint* (the story of Martina Navratilova vs. Chris Evert), *Love Story* (Steffi Graf in her heyday), *Volley of the Dolls* (the women's tennis tour), *Winterset* (indoor tennis), and *King Lear* (the biographies of Ilie Nastase, Jimmy Connors, and John McEnroe).

Now I was ready to write my slogans. Linesmen ready? Here they are:

- Shake hands with our racquet.

- We're dedicated to faultless services in New Hampshire.

- We deliver a smashing opportunity.

- Our service will improve your service.

Apparently the panel of judges reacted like a cross court. They wondered what the deuce I was doing writing these base lines. So as a backhanded compliment, they declared as the winner my fifth slogan, the one that didn't have any pun in it at all: "The sport for a lifetime in the state for a lifetime." And why not? It was the one with the American twist!

Winning a slogan contest—and, for my labors, a can of tennis balls—isn't the only reward for a lifetime of being a jack-of-all-trades, master of pun. Early in 1989, I received a delicious invitation: "The International Save the Pun Foundation (ISPF) cordially invites you to the Fourth Annual Punsters Dinner at Mareva's Restaurant in Chicago. Special guest speaker John Crosbie, Founder and Cheerman of the Bored, and Punster of the Year, Richard Lederer. Come pun, come all!"

Accompanying the invitation was a map of "Oh Pun Territory," marked by such features as Lord's Prairie, Forever Moor, Joan Rivers, Gerald and Henry Fjord, Sit-Up-Strait, Lloyd Bridges, Piggy Bank, Oh-Say-Can-You-Sea, Sexual Peak, Dis-a-Point, Psycho Path, Woody Allen, Gene Autree, W. C. Fields, Air-Plain, and George Bush. The date of the dinner was April Fools' Day, of course.

Yes, Virginia, there really is an International Save the Pun Foundation, a verbal glee club dedicated to wordy causes like preserving the pun as an endangered specious. At the end of 1988 had come a letter from John Crosbie, the presiding gray eminence of the Pun Foundation. Mr. Crosbie's message began, "We are delighted to confirm that this Foundation has chosen you to receive its International Punster of the Year Award for 1989, based on your latest book, *Get Thee to a Punnery*." Thrilled to be designated as Attila the Pun, the top pun of the Western world, I immediately sent off a reply that started with this salutation:

—a rebus that translates into "Dear John Crosbie." You'll get the idea of the whole letter from its first paragraph: "I am all charged up and positively ec-static about the electrifying news that you are planning to socket to me and plugging me to go on the circuit as your Punster of the Year. To re-fuse such a creative outlet would be re-volting to the point of battery. In short, I am de-lighted."

I know. You're a groan-up who thinks that I'm a compulsive puntificator cursed with a pukish, not puckish, imagination. You suspect, I suspect, that I'm a member of the Witless Protection Program. That's all right with me because I amused to wit and always bear in mind the slogan of the International Save the Pun Foundation: "A day without puns is a day without sunshine. There is gloom for improvement."

For all of us who have experienced the loneliness of the long-distance punner, the dinner in Chicago was the farce that lauched a thousand quips. More than two hundred loaded pun-slingers attended, pleased to have so many pun pals to go out wit.

Punnery is largely the trick of compacting two or more ideas within a single word or expression. Punnery challenges us to apply the greatest pressure per square syllable of language. Punnery surprises us by flouting the law of nature that pretends that two things cannot occupy the same space at the same time. Punnery is an exercise of the mind at being concise.

The pun is mightier than the sword, and often sharper— and at the International Save the Pun Foundation festivities, one was much more likely to run into a pun than a sword, as everybody present took a blue ribbin'. The hours fled away because, as one frog said to the other, "Time's fun when you're having flies!" Put that one in your funny pile—and your punny file.

The highlight of the evening was the appearance of the pun made flesh in the person of Joyce Heitler, the president of the Chicago Chapter of the ISPF, who each year comes dressed as the Pun-Up Girl, attired in visual puns that the audience has to decipher. On her head Joyce wore a small weaving mechanism, translating to *frame of mind* or *hair loom*. Her dress was splashed with dots and dashes—*dress code*. On her finger Joyce wore a ring woven out of red hair—*red hair ring*. Around her neck was a lace collar. An easy one: *neck-lace*.

Joyce's most enticing sartorial challenge was that she claimed to be wearing a visual oxymoron—an outward and visible sign of two opposite ideas, such as *jumbo shrimp, pretty ugly*, or *old news*. I spotted an airless inner tube slung over Joyce's shoulder and under her arm. "Flat busted!" I shouted, confident that I had identified the hidden oxymoron. "No, you silly," replied Joyce. "This is at-tire, or, if you wish, a boob tube," at which point this stud re-tired from the competition treading lightly. The oxymoronic solution reposed in the *loose tights* that Joyce was sporting.

Among the evening's delights was a "Rap-Pun Contest" (someone suggested "Rap-Pun-Sel") in which each table of pundits composed a string of puns to rap rhythms. One of the best raps included these verses of poetree. Try reading it aloud rap-aciously:

> *"Oh, Juniper, grow by my side."*
> *The Oak bent down to plant a kiss.*
> *"Some day we will exchange our boughs*
> *And live our lives in wooded bliss."*
>
> *Then Juniper axed her lover Oak*
> *In the morning forest dew,*
> *"Willow bend your limbs abought me,*
> *Maple I wood pine fir yew."*

As Francis Bacon once almost said, without hamming it up, some puns are to be tasted, others to be swallowed, and a few to be chewed and digested. Mareva's is living proof and reproof that a Polish gourmet restaurant is not an oxymoron, and, even though Joyce Heitler proclaimed, "We don't serve soup to nuts," a delicious borscht was brought out, inspiring one punhead to call out, "The heartbeet of America!" The foundation initially thought about holding the dinner in a new restaurant on the moon, a perfect place for a bunch of lunatics. But an investigation revealed that while the Moonie restaurant has great food, it doesn't have any atmosphere.

Then, just for the halibut, the international punsters took a Pole and came up with a number of fishy suggestions for an ideal punsters' menu, a buffet of sole food. Among the tour de farces highest on the scales of effishiency were *salmon rushdie, tuna turner, poisson ivy, bass ackwards, dill pickerel, brain sturgeon, combination lox, porgy best, turn pike,* and *win one for the kipper.* That night the world was our roister. And did you know that a noise annoys an oys-ter?

If you are one to carp about these finny lines, you must be hard of herring.

PUN YOUR WAY TO SUCCESS

Punning is a truly rewording experience. The inveterate (not invertebrate) punster believes that a good pun is like a good steak—a rare medium well done.

Before you start beefing about my spare ribbing, remember that many a meaty pun has been cooked up as advice on how to succeed in the business of life and the life of business. "Don't be a carbon copy of someone else. Make your own impression," punned French philosopher Voltaire. "Even if you're on the right track, you'll get run over if you just sit there," advised humorist Will Rogers centuries later.

Now let's get right to wit:

- The only place where success comes before work is in the dictionary.

- The difference between a champ and a chump is *u*.

- Triumph is just *umph* added to *try*.

- Don't assume. It will make an *ass* out of *u* and *me*.

- Hard work is the yeast that raises the dough.

- The best vitamin for making friends is B-1.

- Break a bad habit—drop it.

- Patience is counting down without blasting off.

- Patience requires a lot of wait.

- Minds are like parachutes: They function only when open.

- To keep your mind clean and healthy, change it every once in a while.

- You can have an open mind without having a hole in your head.

"Big shots are only little shots that keep on shooting," observed British writer Christopher Morley. Here are some more punderful maxims that merit a blue ribbin'. Sharpen your pun cells and start taking notes:

- One thing you can give and still keep is your word.

- A diamond is a chunk of coal that made good under pressure.

- When the going gets tough, the tough get going.

- If the going gets easy, you may be going downhill.

- If you must cry over spilled milk, please try to condense it.

- Don't be afraid to go out on a limb; that's where the fruit is.

- Read the Bible—it will scare the hell out of you.

- The Ten Commandments are not multiple choice.

- Failure is the path of least persistence.

- Life is not so much a matter of position as disposition.

- Of all the things you wear, your expression is the most important.

- If at first you don't succeed, try, try a grin.

"Many people would sooner die than think—and usually they do," lamented British philosopher Bertrand Russell, pun in cheek. Some puns can help us to climb the ladder of success without getting rung out:

- People who never make a mistake never make anything else.

- When you feel yourself turning green with envy, you're ripe to be plucked.

- A smile doesn't cost a cent, but it gains a lot of interest.

- Success is more attitude than aptitude.

- Having a sharp tongue can cut your own throat.

- Learn that the bitter can lead to the better.

- He who throws mud loses ground.

- Hug your kids at home, but belt them in a car.

- Fear is the darkroom where negatives are developed.

- Humans are like steel. When they lose their tempers, they are worthless.

- Don't learn safety rules by accident. Don't be dead to rites.

- There are two finishes for automobiles—lacquer and liquor.

- Learn from the nail. Its head keeps it from going too far.

- He who laughs, lasts.

Even though it's a jungle out there, a real zoo, this collection of beastly puns may help you succeed in a workaday world that depends on survival of the fittest:

- Frogs have it easy. They can eat what bugs them.

- There's nothing in the middle of the road but yellow stripes and dead armadillos.

- Birds have bills too, but they keep on singing.

- Don't be like a lemming. Avoid following the crowd and jumping to conclusions.

- Be like a horse with some horse sense—stable thinking and the ability to say "nay."

- Be like a dog biting its tail. Make both ends meet.

- Be like a giraffe. Stick your neck out and reach higher than all the others.

- Be like a beaver. Don't get stumped; just cut things down to size.

- Be like a lion. Live life with pride and grab the lion's share with might and main.

- Be like an owl. Be wise but still give a hoot.

- Be like a duck. Keep calm and unruffled on the surface, but paddle like crazy underneath.

- Be like the woodpecker. Just keep pecking away until you finish the job. You'll succeed by using your head.

A BILINGUAL PUN

IS TWICE THE FUN

A good pun is its own reword, and bi-lingual puns are twice as rewording as those that stay within the boundaries of a single language. Some of the most pyrotechnic puns have a French twist, into which you can sink your teeth—*bon mot*lars, perhaps:

- Why do the French need only one egg to make an omelet? Because in France, one egg is *un oeuf*.

- Have you stayed at the new luxury hotel in town? It's a site for soirees.

- Have you heard about the student in Paris who spent too much time sitting in a hard chair studying? She got sore buns.

- Have you heard about the milk maid who worked on a really big farm? She had a prominent dairy air.

- *Pas de deux:* the father of twins.

- *Jeanne d'Arc:* a bathroom with no light.

- *Coup de grace:* what a French lawn mower does.

- *Eau de Cologne:* I'll pay for the perfume later.

- *Cul de sac:* sort paper bags.

- *Ma Belle Dame sans merci:* unfriendly telephone operator.

- *S'il vous plait:* not sterling.

- *Soupçon:* dinner's ready.

- *N'est-ce pas:* papa bird.

- A company tried to manufacture prosthetic devices for feline amputees, but found there was no market for the product. You might say that they committed a faux paw.

- A feline kept yacking away inappropriately. Finally, his fellow felines tied an anchor around his legs and threw him into a river. The result: Undue twaddle; cat sank.

- "I hate reading Victor Hugo," said Les miserably.

- Motto of the three musketeers: "En garde, we thrust."

- A class of second graders inadvertently came up with a French pun. After an especially hard day, the teacher sighed aloud, "C'est la vie."

  With one voice the children called out, "La vie!"

- A snail oozed into an automobile showroom, pulled out fifty thousand dollars in crisp bills and ordered a fancy red convertible. "One favor," the snail requested. "Please paint a big S on each of the doors."

  "Sure," said the salesman, "but why would you want that?"

The snail replied: "So that when my friends see me driving down the street, they can all shout, 'Look at the S car go!' "

Great bilingual tropes brighten languages other than French. The all-time prize for transmitting the fullest message with the greatest compactness must go to Sir Charles James Napier. In 1843, Napier quelled an uprising in the Indian province of Sind and announced his triumph via telegram to his commanders in London. All he wrote was the word *Peccavi*.

The Foreign Office broke into cheers. In an age when all gentlemen studied Latin, Napier never doubted that his superiors would remember the first-person past perfect tense of *peccare*—and would properly translate his message as "I have sinned."

Here are some polyglot plays on words that should be understandable, even without much knowledge of a second language:

- At an Italian restaurant I don't know whether I'm antipasto or provolone.

- Have you heard about the liberated Irish woman? Her name was Erin Go Braless.

- When a pig roast takes place in England, several boars are needed to feed the hungry, but in Russia, one Boris Gudonov.

- Have you heard about the Chinese restaurant that stays open twenty-four hours a day? It's called Wok Around the Clock.

- Have you visited the Jewish section of India's capital city? It's called Kosher Delhi.

- Does that last pun get a standing oy vaytion?

- No question about it. Adolf Hitler created a terrible führer.

- What do you call a secondhand clothing store in India? Whose Sari Now?

- When Brutus told Julius Caesar that he had eaten a whole squab, Caesar replied, "Et tu, Brutè."

- A classics teacher in Maine owns a boat that he's christened *Navego*, which is Latin for "I sail" and pronounced, "Now we go."

- The space station Mir has had so many collisions because objects in Mir are closer than they appear.

- Mexican weather report: Chili today, hot tamale.

- A Mexican visiting the United States went into a store to buy a pair of socks. He spoke no English, and the clerk didn't know a word of Spanish. Through pantomime, the Mexican tried to explain what he needed, without much success. The clerk brought out shoes, then tried sneakers, then slippers, then laces—all to no avail.

  Finally, he came out of the stockroom with a pair of socks, and the Mexican exclaimed, "Eso sí que es!"

  Said the exasperated clerk, "Well, for crying out loud. If you could spell it, why didn't you say so in the first place?"

- There are many stories related to the sinking of the *Titanic*. Some have just come to light due to the success of the recent movie. For example, most people don't know that back in 1912, Hellmann's mayonnaise was manufactured in England. The *Titanic* was carrying twelve thousand jars of the condiment scheduled for delivery in Veracruz, Mexico, which was to be the next port of call for the great ship after New York City.

The Mexican people were eagerly awaiting delivery and were disconsolate at the loss. So much so that they declared a national day of mourning, which they still observe today. It is known, of course, as Sinko de Mayo.

- On a Monday morning, the mayor of New York gathered reporters and announced the rejuvenation of the ailing New York City transit system. The *New York Daily News* reporter covering the story realized that the situation was too good to be true. His headline read: SICK TRANSIT'S GLORIOUS MONDAY.

- Chico Marx once took umbrage upon hearing someone exultantly exclaim, "Eureka!"

  Chagrined, Chico shot back, "You doan smella so good yourself!"

FACE THE MUSIC

Larry Lobster and Sam Clam were best friends. They did everything together. The only difference between them was that Larry was the nicest lobster ever, and Sam, well let's just say he was not so virtuous. Larry and Sam did so much together that they even died together. Larry went to heaven and Sam went to hell.

One day Saint Peter came up to Larry and said, "Larry, you know you are the nicest lobster we ever had up here. Everyone likes you, but you seem to be a bit depressed. Tell me what's bothering you. Maybe I can help."

Larry replied, "Well, don't get me wrong, Pete. I like it up here and everything, but I really miss my good friend Sam Clam. We used to do everything together."

Saint Peter pitied Larry and said, "I tell you what. I can arrange it so that you can go down to hell tomorrow and visit Sam for twenty-four hours. How does that sound?" This made Larry very happy. He rose bright and early the next morning and grabbed his wings, his harp, his halo, and got on the elevator to hell.

When the doors opened, he was met by Sam. They hugged each other and off they went. You see, in hell Sam owned a disco. They spent the day there together and had a great time. At the end of the day, Larry and Sam said their good-byes, and up Larry elevated. When he stepped off the elevator, he was greeted by Saint Peter, who blocked the doorway to heaven. "Larry Lobster," Saint Peter asked, "didn't you forget something?"

Larry looked around and said, "No, I don't think so. I have my halo and my wings."

"Yes, but what about your harp?"

Larry gasped and said, "Oh dear, I left my harp in Sam Clam's disco!"

You've just been the victim of a setup pun, a conspiracy of narrative and wordplay. In setup punnery, the punster contrives an imaginary situation that leads up to a climax cunningly and punningly based upon a well-known expression or title. Some of the most punderful setups reach a foreordained conclusion that consists of a line from a popular song. Tony Bennett would turn over in his bed at the ingenuity of the prize specimen that just kicked off this harmonious anthology of noteworthy puns.

Hey, I don't want to blow my own horn or trumpet my accomplishments, but I am feeling fit as a fiddle, and I don't fiddle around or play second fiddle to anyone. I don't wish to harp on this subject or chime in on your conversation, but I never play it by ear and never give you a second-string performance. I don't ever soft-pedal any aspect of the English language, and I always pull out all the stops. I, your unsung hero, will never lay on you too much sax and violins. Rather, I wish simply to drum up enthusiasm for musical wordplay.

I really do know my brass from my oboe, so I hope that the five additional classics that you are about to listen to will be music to your ears:

A father waited in line with his daughter Shelly for the chance to sign the White House guest book. Impatiently the little girl pushed in front of a nun to get her turn. The father restrained his daughter with the admonition, "Wait till the nun signs, Shelly!"

Rudolph, a dedicated Russian Communist and important rocket scientist, was about to launch a large satellite. His wife, a fellow scientist at the base with a background in meteorology, urged Rudolph to postpone the launch because, she asserted, a hard rain would soon fall. Their collegial disagreement soon escalated into a furious argument that Rudolph closed by shouting, "Rudolph the Red knows rain, dear!"

A group of chess-playing fanatics would gather each morning in the hotel lobby to brag about their greatest victories. Came a day when the hotel manager barred the group from the lobby—because he couldn't stand to hear a bunch of chess nuts boasting in an open foyer.

One of the greatest men of the twentieth century was Mahatma Gandhi. His denial of the earthly pleasures included the fact that he never wore anything on his feet. Moreover, he ate so little that he developed delicate health and bad breath. The result was a super callused fragile mystic hexed by halitosis.

Here is what I believe is the most adroit of all melodious setup puns. I make this claim because of the way the *punch* line, syllable by syllable, skips along right up next to the original song line:

Cowboy singer Roy Rogers went bathing in a creek. Along came a cougar and, attracted by the smell of new leather, began nibbling on one of Roy's brand-new boots, which were sitting by the edge of the water. Dale Evans entered the scene and, noting the critter chomping her husband's footwear, fired her trusty rifle in the air, scaring the cougar away.

Then she turned to her husband and asked, "Pardon me, Roy. Was that the cat that chewed your new shoe?"

THE NAME IS THE GAME

Has Elvis Presley achieved such immortality because *Elvis lives* is an anagram of itself?

The first name of the man who tried to put the world between Iraq and a hard place reposes in the following palindromic statement, one that can be read the same forwards and backwards: DRAT SADDAM, A MAD DASTARD!

If Ella Fitzgerald married Darth Vader, she'd be Ella Vader. If Rosemary De Camp married William Kunstler, she'd be Rosemary De Camp Kunstler.

H. Rider was Haggard, but Thomas was Hardy. Oscar was Wilde, but Thornton was Wilder. Dame May was Whitty, but John Greenleaf was Whittier.

William Shakespeare must have written the works of William Shakespeare because who else possesses a name whose letters can be juggled (anagrammed) into four right-on statements?

I SWEAR HE'S LIKE A LAMP.
WE ALL MAKE HIS PRAISE.
HAS WILL A PEER, I ASK ME?
AH, I SPEAK A SWELL RIME.

Take it from RIDDLER REACHER—an anagram for *Richard Lederer*. It's fun to play around with people's names. The incorrigible punster (please don't incorrige!) can't help but notice that some people have first or last names that sound like lowercase words, such as Ulysses Grant, Oliver Sacks, and Iris Murdoch.

Special fun lurks in those people who possess both first and last names that sound like lowercase words. One might call Johnny Cash "coins collected from a pay toilet," Norman Mailer "a French postman," Eartha Kitt "gardening tools," and Doug Flutie "a buried flautist."

Now let's focus on movie stars whose names are also doubly blessed. From the punny clues below, give the name of each movie star. *Example:* "Scarlet clothing fasteners" = Red Buttons. Hint: The answers, which repose in "Answers to Games and Quizzes" (page 287), are in alphabetical order by last name.

1. Christmas fruit 2. boyfriend spans 3. toilet confection 4. transport the workout space 5. car pursuit
6. valley nearby 7. Christmas scaredy cat 8. steal the blackbird 9. male cat on a ship trip 10. male goat quartz
11. toilet crane 12. tiny car operator 13. Egyptian ruler's spigot 14. toilet meadows 15. transport the scholarship
16. chromosome slicer 17. talkative fog 18. cabin in the sky 19. what fishermen live on 20. stony automobile
21. pop-top collector 22. jewel bargeman 23. steal from

the bottom 24. thoughtful conqueror 25. she wagers modestly

26. unpedigreed male alley cat 27. toilet agony 28. nail fruit seed 29. stream protectors 30. crimson bones

31. tear ripped 32. solder after Monday 33. crazier chromosome 34. coldest season at the beach 35. tastefully attired forest

"... AND GLADLY TEACH"

TEACHERS CHANGE LIVES

One of my favorite newspaper corrections reads: "It was incorrectly reported last Friday that today is T-shirt Appreciation Week. In fact, it is actually Teacher Appreciation Week."

In 1985, the National Education Association and National PTA set aside the first full week in May as a time to honor teachers and show respect for their profession. Every day should be devoted to Teacher Appreciation and made a time to recognize members of the most unheralded, labor-intensive, multitasking, exhausting, income-challenged, and rewarding of all professions. Indicative of all this is a recent survey that showed that 71 percent of teachers in U.S. public school systems purchased books and supplies with their own money to cover textbook shortages.

Having been an inmate in the House of Correction (aka an English teacher) for twenty-eight years, I'm biased of course. To George Bernard Shaw's mean sneer, "He who can, does. He who cannot, teaches," I would oppose Lee Iacocca's

"In a truly rational world, the best of us would be teachers, and the rest of us would do something else." I truly believe that teachers deserve the nice things people say about them:

And gladly wolde he learn and gladly teche.
—Geoffrey Chaucer

No bubble is so iridescent or floats longer than one blown by a beloved teacher.
—Sir William Osler

Teaching is not a lost art, but the regard for it is a lost tradition.
—Jacques Barzun

He who opens a school door, closes a prison.
—Victor Hugo

By learning you will teach, by teaching you will learn.
—Latin proverb

Only the educated are free.
—Epictetus

Education is light; lack of it is darkness.
—Russian proverb

The man who can make hard things easy is the educator.
—Ralph Waldo Emerson

The mediocre teacher tells. The good teacher explains. The superior teacher demonstrates. The great teacher inspires.
—William Arthur Ward

Teachers, who educate children, deserve more honor than parents, who merely gave them birth; for the latter provided mere life, while the former ensures a good life.
—Aristotle

All one can really leave one's children is what's inside their heads. Education, in other words, and not earthly possessions, is the ultimate legacy, the only thing that cannot be taken away.
—Wernher von Braun

Teachers are expected to reach unattainable goals with inadequate tools. The miracle is that at times they accomplish this impossible task.
—Halm G. Ginot

When love and skill work together, expect a masterpiece.
—John Ruskin

A teacher affects eternity. No one can tell where his influence stops.
—Henry Brooke Adams

To me the sole hope of human salvation lies in teaching.
—George Bernard Shaw (Yes, the same GBS.)

Speaking of salvation, Saint Peter hears a knocking at the gates of heaven and calls out, "Who's there?"

"It is I," a voice responds.

"Oh no, not another English teacher," sighs Saint Peter.

Saint Peter welcomes the teacher into heaven and says he will show her to where she will reside for eternity.

The first neighborhood is lovely—exquisite mansions set

in gorgeous grounds. The teacher asks if this is where she will live, but Saint Peter says it's just for lawyers. The teacher rolls her eyes and sighs.

They float on, and the teacher sees another neighborhood that is even more beautiful. The mansions are even more lavish. People stroll park lawns, socialize, and play golf on a beautiful course. Everyone is having a terrific time. Again she inquires if this is where she will live, but Saint Peter says it's for doctors.

On through the clouds they drift and soon come to a third neighborhood. It is the most luminous of all. Added to the grandest mansions, parks, pools, and golf courses are magnificent libraries, schools, theaters, and concert halls. Saint Peter tells the teacher this will be her new home in heaven. The teacher is thrilled, but she notices that no one is around, and all the mansions seem to be empty. She asks Saint Peter where everyone is. Don't many teachers make it to heaven? Saint Peter announces that yes, there are lots of teachers in heaven, and they won't return until the next day. They are all in hell attending an in-service training session.

Back on earth, almost a half century ago, during the administration of Dwight D. Eisenhower, James Michener, author of *Hawaii, The Source,* and other megasellers, was invited to a celebrity dinner at the White House. Michener declined to attend and explained: "Dear Mr. President: I received your invitation three days after I had agreed to speak a few words at a dinner honoring the wonderful high school teacher who taught me how to write. I know you will not miss me at your dinner, but she might at hers."

Michener received a handwritten reply from the understanding Ike: "In his lifetime a man lives under fifteen or sixteen presidents, but a really fine teacher comes into his life but rarely. Go and speak at your teacher's dinner."

A Middle Eastern legend tells of a sparrow that was lying on its back with its legs up in the middle of a road. Along came a horseman who, seeing the sparrow, dismounted and asked, "Why are you lying here on your back in the middle of the road?"

"Because I have heard that the heavens will fall today."

"I see. And you think you can hold them up with those spindly legs of yours?"

And the bird answers: "One must do what one can."

Blessed be the teachers. They do what they can, and then they do more than they can. Amalgams of scholars, mentors, counselors, coaches, traffic controllers, and baby-sitters, they march in the company of secular saints. May their tribe thrive and multiply.

TEACHING IN GHETTOBURG

Nine score and fourteen years ago our white forefathers brought
forth upon this continent a black race of slaves, deceived in liberty
and dedicated to the supposition that all men are created equal and
treated equal, except black men.

Thus wrote one of my tenth-grade students in an essay
titled "The Ghettoburg Address" during my sabbatical year of
teaching English at Simon Gratz High School, an inner city
school in North Philadelphia. In 1955, I had graduated from
West Philadelphia High School; fourteen years later, I took a
one-year leave from St. Paul's School to go home again and
return to the school system that spawned me.

During that school year of 1969–70, I began to discover
the political realities of school in the ghetto and to see how
the setup produced a lot of built-in failure. Gratz sits on the
corner of its boundaries. If you happened to live across the
street (in which case you might be white or middle class), you
didn't go to Gratz. Whether or not gerrymandering afore-

thought was at work, our student body was ninety-nine-and-forty-four-one-hundredths percent African American (we had three Asians and one Caucasian on our rolls) and 95 percent poor, removing the kind of social mix that is a crucial factor in lifting achievement levels. While two other high schools sat underused just outside our territory, Gratz bulged with forty-five hundred students who were processed in two sequential shifts—7:50 A.M. to 12:05 P.M., then 12:15 P.M. to 4:30 P.M. Our kids were with us at least an hour less than most youngsters in other schools, and they spent their shifts going straight through classes without any breaks for lunch, study hall, or socializing. When two of my "slow" classes came to me each day for sixth and seventh periods (3:10 P.M. to 4:30 P.M.), many were numbed, hungry, and eager to get out of the building.

Apathy, not violence, was the most formidable opponent to education at Gratz. Our average daily attendance was 68 percent, and once inside the building, the student body collectively cut thousands of classes a week. Only half of our tenth graders returned to Gratz the next year and only one in three graduated from the school.

Still, as I recollect in the tranquillity of more than three decades after my experiences at Gratz, I feel some joy. If education means change and the discovery of psychic mobility, I know that some of my students had at least a day of education in my classroom. I know that I touched some of my students and that they touched each other. I remember the faces, often vacant, hostile, and weary of the ritual. But almost every day something beautiful happened on some of the faces, and the heavens, rather than falling, opened. What happened often had to do with language.

I wanted my students to know that language is not a set of thou shalt's out there, but an instinct in here, as natural as breathing and digesting and mating—a part of people, not apart from them, a making of meanings in the brain, a gathering of meanings from the world, an offering of meanings to the world. In the service of this philosophy, the core of my writing program was a weekly journal, ungraded and risk free, in which each student began not with an exterior assignment but with him or herself. I stressed that bold and sincere thinking, and even sheer quantity, would count more than mechanics. In response there poured forth talent so rich and vast that it made my blood quicken:

> I remember once when I was stopped by the fuzz for suspicion of snatching some lady's pocketbook. So he took me down to the 39th police station, and it seemed like it was two hours while I was down there, and you talk about somebody being hungry. Man, I was ready to eat the cigarettes in my pocket.

> When the freedom, or should I say bush, came out, the pink man did not like this one bit. And he was very mad when our females started wearing it. Want to know why? He is angry because some of our women are not spending the money on all that possum fat. VO-5 pinkies are mad because they can't go home and tell their families about "that dumb nigger lady," as they would say it, who has bought $10 worth of hair lard.

The sense of relationship to the environment, what our principal called the students' sense of "fate control," is crucial to their ability to learn. What happened to my students' sense of life's promises, I asked myself, when only one in fifteen had a room of their own at home and only one in ten a room where they could go to study? Again and again in their writing my students questioned their place in and control over the universe, as in these haiku poems:

Why have I risen
From the bosom of life
Into this world of hatred?

I am lost in a river—
The river of prejudice.
What am I doing here?

The birds sing with beauty.
Blood stains the turning earth.
What does it all mean?

Where is the key to education?
What will I find
When the door is opened?

Why must I hold this gun?
Why must I kill my brother?
Is God alive?

And this quatrain:

Mama's sick.
Daddy's drunk.
Brother's in jail
And I just flunked.

And this free verse:

Thoughts
Running freely
Skipping, hopping,
Never stopping.
Life,
Death,
Heroin, meth.

I wanted my students to know that Black English is a major dialect spoken by a great number of Americans of African descent, that Black English has a long, rich history that began in Africa when people from many villages were transported to American slave markets, and that many of the distinctive forms of Black English have been identified as residues of West African languages.

Since my year of teaching at Simon Gratz High School, Black English has become better known as Ebonics, a term that blends the words *ebony* and *phonics* and burst upon the American consciousness during the Oakland School Board controversy in 1996. The board voted to recognize Ebonics as a distinct language, with its own vocabulary, syntax, and usage, and to create a program to train teachers to understand students who speak Ebonics. The decision provoked an outcry from public figures as diverse as media rightist Rush Limbaugh and African-American poet Maya Angelou, conservative William J. Bennett and the liberal Jesse Jackson.

I believe that Ebonics is a dialect, not a language, because Ebonics speakers and standard English speakers pretty much understand each other. But Ebonics is a dialect with a difference. While most other dialects are confined to specific geographical regions, Ebonics is shared by many African Americans living throughout the United States. And while the majority of regional dialects are relatively free from social stigma, Ebonics has been branded as an inferior form of standard English—the product of lazy lips and lazy minds.

Yet Ebonics is a vessel that fully serves the needs of its users. Its grammar is just as elaborate, rule-governed, and internally consistent as that of standard English. The meaning of "He didn't do nothing" is perfectly understood by all Ebonics speakers and by standard English speakers as well. In "They bad kids" the subject-verb relationship is quite clear, and in "You don' stop messin' wif me, I'm gonna hit upside yo head," the *if-then* logic is perfectly evident, even if not stated. "My sister sick" means that she is sick right now but it won't last very long, while "My sister be sick" indicates a continuing, long-term illness. Such a subtle distinction is more easily and concisely communicated in Ebonics than in standard English.

As writer Ishmael Reed makes clear, the use of Ebonics indicates neither a lack of education nor an inability to speak in other tongues: "You not gone make me give up Black English. When you ask me to give up Black English you askin me to give up my soul. But for reasons of commerce, transportation, and hassleless mobility in everyday life, I will talk to 411 in the language both the operator and I can understand."

Still, it was only fair to warn my students that in certain contexts someone, perhaps a prospective employer, might make a damaging judgment about a double negative or an *a* before a noun beginning with a vowel, as in "a ink pen." Those who wanted to get a job outside their community would have to think about learning the mainstream, standard dialect and becoming, so to speak, bidialectal. At the same time I asked my students to pray with me for the rapid withering of that so very comforting, so uniquely human myth: *We* talk right and *they* don't. Would anyone want to snuff out such "non-standard" expressions as "I offed him," "I just snapped out," and "She runs her mouth too much"?

Such sentences suggest an integral part of my students' writing that constantly delighted me. We take for granted a convention called "the writing voice" that differs in varying degrees from one's speaking voice, depending on the writer and the task of writing. At Gratz few students employed such an aesthetic distance in their composing.

It is unfortunate that the beautiful oral language of many of my students got clogged up in their pens. But when the style and content were able to traverse that tricky route from mind and spirit to paper, the results were often, as Frantz Fanon describes in *Wretched of the Earth*, "a vigorous style, alive with rhythms, struck through with bursting life; . . . full of color too, bronzed, sunbaked."

As my students found and practiced their voices, they increasingly affirmed their blackness. In celebrating their negritude, in exploring aspects of their consciousness that were in the process of being liberated, and in the combative tone of their writing, my students were acting out the history of black literature in the United States and the rearrangement of political relationships during their lifetimes:

Black Is Beautiful

Black is beautiful.
Beautiful is black.
Let's get together.
That's where it's at.

Black is powerful.
Black is sharp.
Everybody's learning
To be proud of their dark.

Black is colorful.
Black is cool.
We're no nigger children.
We're no fools.

Black is being proud.
Black is black.
Let's stick together
'Cause that's where it's at.

I'm Not a Boy

I've got a name.
Don't call me boy.
I've got a name.
I'm not a walkin' toy.

Try "Mister" or "Sir"
To suit your taste.
But don't call me boy
'Cause you're out of place.

Mother Africa

This is my land.
I've made it so.
With the sweat of my brow
I've helped it grow.

By the laws of man
I should be free.
But the white man's laws
Are as chains to me.

Back Off!

Back off, Whitey,
'Cause Nigger is no longer my name.
Back off Whitey,
'Cause your dog and mine are no longer the same.
Back off Whitey,
'Cause I'm hip to your dehumanizing game.

You Don't Know

When some cracker says,
"You're a good boy,"
You don't know whether to blush
And melt like a stick of butter
Or to just stand there and stink
Like a fresh shit.

My students never let me get hung up on aesthetic abstractions. Either the material overlapped with their realities and needs, or they turned off with unsophisticated visibility. They allowed me a few castles in the air, but early in each building project they demanded foundations underneath. In preparing to study George Orwell's *Animal Farm*, for example, we spent two weeks reading a number of Ethiopian and Greek fables. The students wrote their own fables, taking care to use appropriate animals and appropriate plots to yield a moral that followed from the story. Then we discussed this question: "If you were a modern writer of fables, what aspects of contemporary society would you choose to comment on?" From the discussion to the blackboard went such social problems as gangs, drugs, violence, racial prejudice, cars, cigarettes, and pollution. Finally, the students fashioned their own fables for our time:

The Alligator and the Frog

Once upon a time there lived an alligator and a frog. Each lived on the opposite side of each other. One day they were sitting on a rock and the alligator said, "We the alligators are better than you green and all-colored frogs." And the frog said, "We the frogs are better than you scaly punks." And they just kept it up until they challenged one another.

"All right, you little short sissy, we'll see you and your puny gang tomorrow," said Alligator.

"Your challenge is accepted," said Frog hatefully.

The day arrived and the fight was about to begin. After a five-minute prayer they all began to fight. The frogs were hopping all over the alligators with knives and clubs in their feet, while the alligators were biting and snapping at the frogs with their mouths.

And finally the fight ended and the alligators and the frogs realized that all their leaders had been killed along with others. So from that day on everyone took heed of the killing.

Moral: Gang war—it just don't make no sense.

When we experienced *Animal Farm* itself, our emphasis was on the uses and abuses of power and the malignant growth of discrimination among the animals. During one lesson, we compared the goals and commandments of the Animal Revolution with those of the Black Panther Party: "Any party member found shooting narcotics will be expelled from the party"; "No party member will use, point, or fire a weapon of any kind unnecessarily or accidentally at anyone."

In our next unit we explored the world of Greek mythology. We compared the ancient stories with the Black Muslim myth of the creation of white people by Mr. Yacub, a malevolent, "big-head" scientist, as told in *The Autobiography of Malcolm X*. We saw that the scientific, empirical truth of a myth is not what is most important. What counts is that it furnishes a transcendent set of explanations for a particular group of people, that it fills their lives with sufficient meaning to make their living and striving worthwhile. The students then created their own gods and myths, and many of the writers captured in mythic form a sense of their own existences:

Jason, god of drugs, is a descendent of Linus, god of Laziness. Jason and his followers are very dangerous people. They steal and kill just for money to keep their habit going, and they call to their god Jason to bring them Speed, Monster, and Skag.

Jason is an evil god. After his followers have taken the dope, Jason makes them sick and they need another shot. Many of the followers die from O.D.'s.

Finally, Zeus promised to overthrow Jason by fire. Zeus conjured up one of his biggest fireballs. It struck Jason and that's where we get Sunday.

Teaching at Simon Gratz High School was the best course I ever took. I knew that when I visited the ghetto for one year, I would go there to learn all I could. I tried not to delude myself into thinking that I would be saving any minds and souls. Still, it doesn't seem fair that most of the time I was the one doing all the learning.

HAPPY MEDIA

One well-lit July afternoon, Stu, Chris, and Gary go to the St. Paul's School auditorium to set up their video cameras at various angles to and distances from the long steps in front of the hall. Stu mounts his studio camera for a side view, Chris readies his for straight-ahead shots, Gary plants his inside the hall, atop the balcony and looking down the steps, and Al prepares to rove the set with his portable rig.

Responding to an announcement at lunch, fifty students and teaching staff assemble for an hour to play out the scene. With calm authority, Doug, the director, explains the concept of the action to the assembled throng and sends them to their places. The cameras start.

On the finished videotape, the students are frolicking—dancing, horseplaying, tossing Frisbees. Suddenly "SUDDENLY" flashes on the screen, and the background music changes from light to ominous. The teachers appear, locked in two rigid lines, their lips set tightly, their grim faces begoggled, their heads bedecked with hunting hats. Summer school director

225

Phil Bell, in the role of the czarist general, waves the faculty forward. They advance inexorably, each one thrusting forth a tennis racquet.

The students panic and career wildly down the long steps. The music builds. Dozens of quick cuts: twisted faces, churning legs, plummeting bodies; several shots of Doug frozen in a silent scream.

The first line of pedagogues kneels, raises a column of stringed weapons, and delivers (literally) a volley of tennis balls at the confused kids. Many victims fall dead or wounded. A second line rises above the first and, with deft overhead arcs, bats out another round. More students hit the hard stone of the steps. Amid the tumult, Jeff lifts Bev into his arms and mounts the stairs fearlessly, advancing into the threatening shadow of the waiting faculty forces. "MY CHILD IS WOUNDED" appears on the screen. Another fuzzy fusillade, and Jeff and Bev collapse.

Then a tennis ball strikes Carolyn. The impact jars the baby carriage she has been tending, and the carriage teeters on a step and careers forward. More cuts as the camera follows the carriage and the horrified reactions of the students as the music rises in a grinding crescendo. The forces of tyranny have crushed the innocence of callow frivolity. "STUDY HOURS RE-SUME."

It has been a typical hour in the life of Mass Media, one of the courses that make up the St. Paul's summer school program. Film cognoscenti will recognize the student project as an exercise in parody derived from what may be the most archetypal images in international film, the Odessa steps sequence in Sergei Eisenstein's 1925 silent classic, *The Battleship Potemkin*.

As you know by now, I am an unrepentant, self-confessed

verbivore, a man caught in the web of words. But I have long felt that language consists of more than just words. I have always viewed my beloved teaching tool, the book, as an audiovisual aid, among the first in history.

Of the medium of print Socrates, in *Phaedrus*, complained: "The discovery of the alphabet will create forgetfulness in the learners' souls, because they will not use their memories. They will trust to the external written characters and not remember of themselves." We now know that the book has enriched our memories and perceptions of the human tragedy and comedy. If, like the book, nonprint media can offer students a broader range of stimuli to which they can respond, they will be more likely to communicate and will tell their stories more richly.

Early in my career as an English teacher at St. Paul's School, I saw that my students lived in a culture that was becoming increasingly involved in television, radio, film, tape, and the computer, and that in these media so many of us are finding much of our information and many of our dreams and modes of living.

Nowadays, pop goes our culture. And as that pop culture adds snap and crackle to our everyday parlance, our words and expressions are increasingly brought to us courtesy of a new irreality. Television, radio, film, and advertising make us an offer we can't refuse (*The Godfather*), so we come on down (*The Price Is Right*) and awaaay we go (Jackie Gleason). I mean cowabunga, dude (*The Simpsons*, which took the expression from *Teenage Mutant Ninja Turtles*, which took it from a greeting exchanged by Buffalo Bob Smith and Chief Thunderthud on the *Howdy Doody Show* of the 1950s), just when you thought it was safe (slogan for *Jaws*) to think about language, that all-pervasive and persuasive mediaspeak is baaack (*Poltergeist II*). Now it's the real thing (Coca-Cola) and fingerlickin' good (Kentucky Fried Chicken) to the very last drop (Maxwell House coffee). You may shrug, "Frankly, my dear [verbivore], I don't give a damn" (the ending of *Gone With the Wind*) and "Never mind," but I say, "Excuuuse me" and "Isn't that special?" (from *Saturday Night Live* comedians Gilda Radner, Steve Martin, and Dana Carvey). As Al Jolson exclaimed way back in *The Jazz Singer*, "Wait a minute! Wait a minute! You ain't heard nothing yet!"

We are all immersed in a new media environment, a product of forces dramatically converging in our lifetime. By the time he or she is five years old, the typical American child will have spent more hours in front of a television set than he or she will ever spend in a college classroom. By the time that student graduates from high school, he or she will have spent half again as many hours watching television as he or she will have spent in class.

If language is a system through which we deal with reality, I wanted to become familiar with the languages of the new nonprint media in order to help my students catch and crystallize their new realities. Print is certainly a major part of those realities, but it is scarcely the only mass medium to merit careful study. Communication today consists of an orchestration of print and newer technologies, all part of an emerging media ecosystem. In the service of this philosophy, I founded and taught for thirteen years the Mass Media summer school course at St. Paul's.

For six weeks each summer, about two hundred public and parochial high school students from around New Hampshire come to live at St. Paul's School, each choosing a major course of study from offerings in mathematics, science, history, foreign language and culture, religion, creative arts, and media. The idyllic setting, the abundance of time, and the motivated and gifted boys and girls who voluntarily forgo the leisures of summer to come and imbibe each other's excellence make for a platonically ideal educational environment. As I try to capture the special life of the summer school, and the Mass Media experience in particular, I feel like a small figure on tiptoe holding out a butterfly net and hoping to snare a few significant and colorful moments before they forever fly away.

Mass Media begins with a fire hydrant. It is the middle of the first week, and the students have embarked on their first field experience with video cameras. Their assignment: to film an inanimate object. The purpose is to explore and develop the potential of early video cameras to "record" the world around them. The kids are nervous, inexperienced, and technologically awestruck. For a while, it seems that the best they can venture is to adjust the focus occasionally. Everyone stands three or four feet from the hydrant and obtains the same static, lifeless shot. A few are bold enough to walk around the hydrant, but none dare approach it.

None, that is, until Melanie gets her hands on the camera. Immediately, she goes for the zoom lens and begins to probe every crack and corner of the hydrant. She pans the chain, tries overhead and low-angle shots, homes in on the artifact's ripples and textures, rack focuses from one valve to another, and even shoots through the chain links. As thoroughly as Melanie has worked over the hydrant, she has worked over the class. Everyone catches on; everyone is infected with video fever. The students begin to view technology not as an intimidating force, but as potentially creative and liberating in their lives. Later, while viewing the playback of the class's collective footage, someone says, "I never knew a fire hydrant could be so beautiful."

During the course of the summer, students spend half of each morning learning about the aesthetics of film through a series of short, unconventional films, such as *Begone Dull Care* and *Dream of the Wild Horses*, highly visual experiences that elude literary categorizing and penetrate the consciousness at the deepest levels. The goal here is to open the kids' eyes to the screen as aesthetic surface, not as just a "window" into a story world of pseudoreality. We also trace the early history of film, from the very first film program publicly presented, the Lumiere brothers' series of short subjects screened at Le Grand Café in Paris on December 28, 1895, to a week-long, sequence-by-sequence exploration of Orson Welles's incomparable *Citizen Kane*.

Through reading, writing, discussing, reporting, storyboarding, and field work, we want our students to become "cinemate" as well as literate—to enter into the magical conspiracy of electric and electronic light and darkness; to see, feel, and eat film and tape; to participate in the joyous collectivity of film and video making.

During the second and third weeks of the summer program, the students' growing cinemacy becomes transformed into reality. Now they are free to experiment with miniprojects, media adventures in which the emphasis is more on the process than the product. The Odessa steps sequence by Chris, Stu, and Doug is one such project. Sue, Sheri, and Bev combine to fashion a scratch-and-doodle film, scratching and drawing each frame directly onto a piece of 16-mm clear leader to produce a film made without a camera. To the accompaniment of John Denver's "Teacher I Need You" an animated stick-figure student appears on the screen and bewails the mountain of homework confronting him. Lit by a halo scratched onto the film, Saint Paul enters and pities the poor boy, who wakes up the next morning to find his assignments all done.

Joe works in the school radio station producing a tape of

The Joey K Show, a professional blend of news and music that will be played back during a school lunch break. Melanie and Gerry experiment with video montage, intercutting sequences of student life with clips from violent war films. Carolyn and Sally create a multimedia advertising campaign of their original product, Jock Sox. Ross, our resident artist, works with Super 8 film and makes an exquisite animated film of the Garden of Eden. Chuck and Al play with audio feedback, a process by which music is fed into the back of a television monitor and, with the manipulation of cameras and our production bay, is transmuted directly into abstract video images.

As the students complete their audiovisionary experiments, they decide to join forces in a collective miniproject, a videotape they call "The Great Escape." On the screen, the students are shown staggering under the weight of tremendous workloads and gagging on dining-hall food. They plan and execute an escape from the grounds but are headed off by headmaster Bell, who, stationed at the school gate with whip in hand, lashes them back to the toils of summer school.

After lunch, each project is shown in the common room for all summer school students who care to come. Most do, and the screenings become exceptionally intimate times, sprinkled with sounds of laughter and surprise at what is happening on the television or film screen. Usually the media students mingle with the others, answering questions and discussing their work. In their projects, the students have fallen easily into the roles that best suit their respective talents, and each person is unremittingly available to help a classmate by toting a camera or handling a microphone. They become bonded into a kinetic example of film critic Pauline Kael's observation: "Filmmaking is the greatest collective art form since the building of medieval cathedrals."

On the door of the AViary, as our suite of audiovisual rooms is called, is a picture of a woman's face with the caption PEOPLE ARE MEDIA. Nothing in the course illustrates the co-joining of people and machines better than the crowning Mass Media project—the making of a videotape yearbook of the entire summer school program.*

For the yearbook, most mornings are spent shooting footage in the school chapel and in every summer school class; each afternoon a crew goes out to capture sports action; and the cameras mingle with the evening to record dormitory life, square dances, and cookouts. It is easy to spot the Mass Media students. They are the ones with the strained neck muscles, the ones who look depressed every time something funny or exciting has the temerity to happen when no camera is present to record it, the ones who, it seems, view the world as if through the lens of a camera, the ones who cannot see without first adjusting their horizontal and vertical sync pulses.

The students shoot a total of forty hours of source material, and they log it all. From that forty hours they create a final storyboard consisting of hundreds of cuts and edits. Continuity and transitions begin to accumulate: A triangular beaker in the chemistry lab dissolves into a fishing net from an ecology class field trip; the camera cuts from a student writing musical notes on a blackboard to a teacher writing mathematical symbols on another board in another classroom; an experiment in constructing pyramids of cardboard cylinders in a calculus class transmogrifies into the building up and tumbling down of human pyramids at one of the cookouts. The teachers in the Odessa steps sequence raise their tennis rac-

---

*These were the years of black-and-white, open-reel videotape and long before yearbooks on videotape became commonplace.

quets—and then the scene cuts to the tennis courts and the beginning of a sports sequence. I watch my students evolve into electronic children who are extending their senses and perfecting their intellectual and emotional circuitry.

A race against the clock begins. As graduation nears, the editing facilities glow day and night. Students and staff begin to live in the AViary, and one learns to step over the slumbering bodies. As one student wrote at the end of the course: "Showing the yeartape was like watching three weeks of sweat and tough work go up on display wide open for comment. The feeling is as big a high as you can ever get. I really can't comment much further because the day is hazy with tears of joy and sadness."

"I got out of Mass Media exactly what I paid," wrote one student. "I paid with lack of sleep, with screaming, quietly discussing, laughing, singing, listening, and loving. I know that you have to go through hell to get to heaven. But if you make it, it ain't like any other place you've ever been or ever will be again."

Two nights from the end, the students ask Ann, a college intern in English, to come to the AViary and sing "The Lake Isle of Innisfree," a song she had previously presented in chapel. They stretch out on the floor, and there is total silence but for Ann's bell-clear voice:

> I will arise and go now, and go to Innisfree,
> And a small cabin build there, of clay and wattles made:
> Nine bean-rows will I have there, a hive for the
>   honeybee,
> And live alone in the bee-loud glade.

The mood is relaxed, intimate, contemplative. Ann finishes, and no one moves or speaks. A deep sadness is felt, and the members of the class become aware of a strange fact: They want to finish this yeartape, but to finish will mean the end of their time together.

Next evening, the last of the session, the class videotapes the summer school talent show and stays up much of the night editing the raw footage onto the master tape. Finally the credits are done, and so is our task. Martha, a college intern in the course, sings to the class; some of the students go out to watch the sunrise; and Gary, the other intern, is awakened by a vapor of baby powder dumped on his head.

The kids ask us to take them downtown for a last breakfast, and together we all sit giggling over our eggs and orange juice. Two hours later we go to graduation, string three monitors around the auditorium, jack the sound into the hall speakers, and show the yearbook tape to the other students and their families:

"I still get an incredible feeling every time I think of the yeartape," wrote one student, "because we created that! At sixteen I became a surrogate parent, watching my child grow and mature. That's a corny way to express it, but making something like that has part of you in it."

On the screens, the students see themselves as luminous presences learning and playing in places that have become precious. They will return for a reunion the next June to pass each other's way again, and once more the electronic yearbook will work its magic upon them, rekindling memories grown dim. Everyone will cry. It is always the best moment of the year.

ENGLISH WITH

A RUSSIAN DRESSING

At Senate Square in Saint Petersburg, Russia, my wife and I gaze upon a magnificent bronze statue of Peter the Great, which faces the Neva River. The czar of czars is mounted on a rearing steed that tramples a writhing serpent. The tableau represents the victory of Russia over Sweden in the Northern War.

Our guide and hostess, Tatyana Vereshkina, observes a small crowd of children swarming up and down the stone wave that forms the base of the massive sculpture. In their enthusiasm, the boys and girls often bump against the snake. Tatyana clucks, "Well, I've never seen that before, children playing on the statue. They're going to do some damage there. And look at the parents just standing about and allowing the kids to run wild. That statue used to be cordoned off. But I guess that's what happens when you get democracy."

It is the middle of 1994, and for eleven days I am visiting and teaching in a number of schools in Saint Petersburg. I have been invited to the city by the Centre for Concerned

Teachers and SPELTA (Saint-Petersburg English Language Teachers' Association) to show how instruction in English can be made more fun. During my stay, I work with students from ten-year-old third graders to twenty-one-year-old university students of philology to the teachers themselves.

Saint Petersburg is a city of striking contrasts. On our way from the airport, we see, amid the rows of white birches, billboards for American products. On Nevsky Prospekt, the Champs Elysées of the city, exquisite eighteenth-century palaces sit next to Baskin-Robbins ice cream shops.

Saint Petersburg struggles to recover its splendor, but for now the capital and jewel of the Russian Empire has been badly cracked by the hammer of history. It is a bright, cold day in May, and the clocks are striking thirteen—or fourteen or fifteen—any possible time—because most of the clocks don't work. Heaps of rocks and bricks and tree limbs—all manner of smashed debris—lie everywhere. Most mail doesn't get into or out of Russia. The public dial telephones are battered. The public toilets stink. There are scarcely any trash cans. The ruble lies in rubble, inflating at a 2,000 percent annual rate, sending pensioners into the streets to beg and invoking the specter of the Weimar Republic. Many shops are closed, and rows of temporary kiosks line the streets. Where are the baby carriages? Where are the babies?

During the first day, as I am sitting in the metro, a drunk sways before me, then pitches forward and crashes into my face. Later that day I find my back pocket slashed. Someone seeking a wallet I wasn't carrying. Welcome to Russia.

Tatyana Vereshkina is an assistant principal and English teacher at School 105, one of the schools where I taught. She shares a treasure chest of compositions and artwork from her ten-to-twelve-year-olds. All the hues missing from their lives in the city they pour into their drawings, alive and struck through with bursting color. The quality and imagination of their writing made the head swim and the blood sing:

> We are looking for an ideal teacher of English. So we decided to place an advertisement in the paper "The Sunday Mirror" saying what qualities the teacher should possess.
>
> First of all, the teacher should be competent. That means that she/he should have advanced knowledge of languages, as well as the skill to manage children. The teacher should also be a pleasant person to deal with—bright and witty.
>
> Besides, the teacher should be not only mentally fit but also physically fit to enjoy playing with children. And the last quality but not the least one—to be patient. Is there any ideal teacher of that kind?

I trust you'll agree that this little essay would earn a solid grade in most of our junior high schools. It happens to have been written by Dmitri Amahin, a ten-year-old third former at School 105. Despite severe shortages of books, blackboards, and audiovisual bells and whistles, Russian students certainly do learn their English language. Amid the drab devastation, bankrupt infrastructure, and shards of broken philosophies that haunt Saint Petersburg glows an abiding respect and re-markable passion for English. Russia has more English teachers than the United States has students of Russian. English has long been the most popular foreign language taught in the former Soviet Union and is required for most Russian pupils and students. Typically, pupils start learning English in the first, second, or third form, studying the language for three hours each week. In the upper levels, they increase their English immersion to six hours each week, including Saturday mornings.

The first day I arrive at School 105 I am welcomed by the fifth-form boys and girls in the Friendship Club. The club adviser, Valentina Frantseva, tells me her story: "I went to school in Kazakhstan, just after the war. My father came home from the front, and I was afraid of him. Then I was afraid of the children in my class. The teachers were so strict that they wouldn't let you go to the bathroom. At that moment I concluded that I should be a teacher when I grew up and that I would be kind to my pupils. But I didn't know what subject.

"Then, a new teacher appeared in our fifth grade. She was young and pretty and just out of college, and she spoke a tongue that no one understood. It was like music. It was English! And that was when I decided to become an English teacher."

Valentina takes the children through their English language paces in circle games that involve every student in the room:

"I am twelve years old. How old are you?"

"I am eleven years old. How old are you?"

"Have you been to Moscow?"

"Yes, I have been to Moscow and the Caucasus. Where have you been?"

"I have been to the Urals. Where have you been?"

"What is your hobby?"

"My hobby is drawing. What is your hobby?"

"My hobby is all kinds of sports. What is your hobby?"

"My hobby is collecting stamps. What is your hobby?"

"My hobby is reading all kinds of books. What is your hobby?"

And on it goes in clear, articulate English with barely an accent. Then the children perform two plays for me—*Robin Hood* and *Little Red Riding Hood*—complete with handmade costumes, hand-painted sets, and a genuine understanding of the lines the young actors delivered: "Once upon a time, there was a little girl who had a new pair of red shoes. She also had a grandmother who was very fond of her." I note that both texts are Walt Disney versions of the classic tales. Ah, American iconography.

Higher up in the Russian educational system English blooms. Katya Zarabova, a seventeen-year-old senior at School 105, is often our guide around Saint Petersburg. Each day she plies us with questions about the English language from a list she compiles from her reading: "Why do you say, 'Hi, there' when the person is nearby? Shouldn't it be 'Hi, here'?" "What is the origin of *OK*?" "Why do you call them blue-chip stocks?" "What is a jeep, and how did it get its name?" "What does 'total happening' mean?" "What's the difference between *convince* and *persuade*?"

Katya explains, "I began to study English because my older brother listened to American music, and I wanted to understand the words. Russian has a hard sound to it, but I like English because it is very soft. Speaking English is like chewing gum.

"A lot of English words you can already recognize in Russian—*OK, computer, toaster, mixer, coffee, Coca-Cola,* and *businessman.* And English is all through our sports—*football, dribble, basketball, baseball, volleyball, interview, derby,* and *champion.* Most of the kids like to use English words in their speech, especially slang words like *wow, oops, cool, awesome,* and *yeah* for *yes.* The more you use, the more popular you are."

Included in Tatyana Vereshkina's cache of pupil compositions is a story by Irene Kosmina, a ten-year-old third former, about a drawing room, with a "big, bright carpet," under which live an imaginary horse and tiger:

> The animals are afraid of the volcano in the corner of the room. It has a special kind of power. Sometimes it has eruptions. The animals can hear loud sounds of music, cries of people, and some other things. They know that people call that volcano a TV set. The horse and the tiger are happy that they have Sheila as a friend. She is a real friend, not imaginary.

What will happen when television starts erupting in Russian homes? Will children still be able to speak and write and act in English with such engaging maturity? Will three to five thousand people still come to the National Library reading room each day? Will one continue to see row upon row of riders sitting in the metro reading books? If American-style capitalism and prosperity truly triumph, what will be the fate of the astonishing verbalness of Russian culture?

THE GLAMOUR
OF GRAMMAR

CONAN THE GRAMMARIAN

The owner of a small zoo lost two of his prize animal attractions in a fire. To order another pair, he wrote a letter to a zoological supply company: "Dear Sirs: Please send me two mongooses."

That didn't sound quite right, so he began again with "Dear Sirs: Please send me two mongeese."

Still not sure of that plural either, he made this third attempt: "Dear Sirs: Please send me a mongoose. And, while you're at it, please send me another mongoose."

Many people throughout our land are like the zoo owner, unsure about their usage and fearful of public embarrassment. These needy souls often call on me to make Solomonic judgments about word choice and sentence structure. Sometimes their conceptions of grammar and usage bring to my mind the image of another animal.

In colleges and universities, students from time to time lead a cow upstairs and into an administrator's office. The prank is popular because while you can lead a cow upstairs, you can't lead it downstairs. I know a number of cows like this. They're the bogus usage rules that self-appointed grammarians herd into our national consciousness. It isn't long before we can't get them—the pundits and their rules—out.

One of the most hefty and intractable bovines is that of the use of a preposition to end a sentence. The rule banishing terminal prepositions from educated discourse was invented by the late-seventeenth-century British critic and poet John Dryden, who reasoned that *preposito* in Latin means something that "comes before" and that prepositions in Latin never appear at the end of a sentence. Dryden even went so far as to reedit his own works in order to remove the offending construction. A bevy of prescriptive grammarians have been preaching the dogma ever since.

Unfortunately, Dryden neglected to consider two crucial points. First, the rules of Latin don't always apply to English. There exist vast differences between the two languages in their manner of connecting verbs and prepositions. Latin is a language of cases, English a language of word order. In Latin, it is physically impossible for a preposition to appear at the end of a sentence. Second, the greatest writers in English, before and after the time of Dryden, have freely ended sentences with prepositions. Why? Because the construction is a natural and graceful part of our English idiom. Here are a few examples from the masters:

> *Fly to others that we know not of.*
> —William Shakespeare

> *We are such stuff | As dreams are made on.*
> —William Shakespeare

Conan the Grammarian

Houses are built to live in, not to look on.
—Francis Bacon

What a fine conformity would it starch us all into.
—John Milton

. . . soil good to be born on, good to live on, good to die for and to be buried in.
—James Russell Lowell

All words are pegs to hang ideas on.
—Henry Ward Beecher

The final preposition is one of the glories of the English language. If we shackle its idioms and muffle its music with false rules, we diminish the power of our language. If we rewrite the quotations above to conform to Dryden's edict, the natural beauty of our prose and verse is forced to bow before a stiff mandarin code of structure. "Fly to others of whom we know not"; "All words are pegs upon which to hang ideas"—now the statements are artificial (people simply don't talk like that) and, in most cases, wordier.

The most widely circulated tale of the terminal preposition involves Sir Winston Churchill, one of the greatest of all English prose stylists. As the story goes, an officious editor had the audacity to "correct" a proof of Churchill's memoirs by revising a sentence that ended with the outlawed preposition. Sir Winston hurled back at the editor a memorable rebuttal: "This is the sort of errant pedantry up with which I will not put!"

A variation on this story concerns a newspaper columnist who responded snappily to the accusation that he was uncouthly violating the terminal preposition "rule": "What do you take me for? A chap who doesn't know how to make full use of all the easy variety the English language is capable of? Don't you know that ending a sentence with a preposition is an idiom many famous writers are very fond of? They realize it's a colloquialism a skillful writer can do a great deal with. Certainly it's a linguistic device you ought to read about."

For the punster there's the setup joke about the prisoner who asks a female guard to marry him on the condition that she help him escape. This is a man attempting to use a proposition to end a sentence with.

Then there's the one about the little boy who had just gone to bed when his father comes into the room carrying a book about Australia. Surprised, the boy asks: "What did you bring that book that I wanted to be read to out of from about Down Under up for?"

Now that's a sentence out of which you can get a lot.

My favorite of all terminal preposition stories involves a boy attending public school and one attending private school who end up sitting next to each other in an airplane. To be friendly, the public schooler turns to the preppie and asks, "What school are you at?"

The private schooler looks down his aquiline nose at the public school student and comments, "I happen to attend an institution at which we are taught to know better than to conclude sentences with prepositions."

The boy at public school pauses for a moment and then says: "All right, then. What school are you at, dingbat!" (In other versions of this joke, the last word is saltier than *dingbat*.)

Joining the preposition rule in the rogues' gallery of usage enormities is the split infinitive. "Many years ago, when I was a junior in Thornton Academy in Saco, Maine, I was instructed never, under pain of sin, to split an infinitive," wrote one of my column readers. Note the expression "under pain of sin." It speaks of the priestly power of the English teacher to interpret the verbal nature of the universe and to bring down from some kind of Mount Sinai commandments for the moral and ethical use of the Word.

A split infinitive ("to better understand," "to always disagree") occurs when an adverb or adverbial construction is placed between *to* and a *verb*. In a famous *New Yorker* cartoon, we see Captain Bligh sailing away from the *Bounty* in a rowboat and shouting, "So, Mr. Christian! You propose to unceremoniously cast me adrift?" The caption beneath the drawing reads: "The crew can no longer tolerate Captain Bligh's ruthless splitting of infinitives."

When infinitives are cleft, some schoolmarms, regardless of sex or actual profession, become exercised. Once again we confront the triumph of mandarin decree over reality, of mummified code over usage that actually inhales and exhales—another passionate effort by the absolutists to protect the language from the very people who speak it.

No reputable authority on usage, either in England or in the United States, bans the split infinitive, and major writers— Philip Sidney, John Donne, Samuel Johnson, Samuel Coleridge, Emily Brontë, Matthew Arnold, Thomas Hardy, Benjamin Franklin, Abraham Lincoln, Oliver Wendell Holmes, Henry James, and Willa Cather (to name a dozen out of thousands)—have been blithely splitting infinitives ever since the early fourteenth century. Thus, when I counsel my readers and listeners to relax about splitting infinitives, I am not, to slightly paraphrase *Star Trek*, telling them to boldly go where no one has gone before. Several studies of modern literary and journalistic writing reveal that a majority of newspaper and magazine editors would accept a sentence using the words "to instantly trace" and that the infinitive is cleft in 19.8 percent of all instances where an adverb appears.

The prohibition of that practice was created in 1762 out of whole cloth by one Robert Lowth, an Anglican bishop and self-appointed grammarian. Like Dryden's antiterminal-preposition rule, Lowth's anti-infinitive-splitting injunction is founded on models in the classical tongues. But there is no precedent in these languages for condemning the split infinitive because in Greek and Latin (and all the other romance languages) the infinitive is a single word that is impossible to sever.

Like Winston Churchill, writers George Bernard Shaw and James Thurber had been stylistically hassled by certain know-it-alls once too often. Shaw struck back in a letter to the *Times* of London: "There is a busybody on your staff who devotes a lot of time to chasing split infinitives. I call for the immediate dismissal of this pedant. It is of no consequence whether he decides to go quickly or to quickly go or quickly to go. The important thing is that he should go at once." With typical precision, concision, and incision, Thurber wrote to a meddlesome editor, "When I split an infinitive, it is going to damn well stay split!"

I'm pleased to announce that a closely guarded secret can now be revealed. Working in a remote area of a top-secret grammar complex, a team of linguistic scientists has succeeded in splitting the infinitive. They placed a stockpile of fissionable gerunds and radio-active participles, encased in leaden clichés to prevent con-fusion, in a machine of their own invention called the infinitron. The effect of the bombardment is to dissociate the word to from its main verb until at length an adverb splits an infinitive and is glowingly ejected from the infinitron. But not to worry. The only explosions emanate from Bishop Robert Lowth and his spiritual progeny—those whom Henry W. Fowler, in his *A Dictionary of Modern English Usage*, describes as people who "betray by their practice that their aversion to the split infinitive springs not from instinctive good taste, but from the tame acceptance of the misinterpreted opinions of others."

Why is the alleged syntactical sin of splitting infinitives committed with such frequency? Primarily because in modern English adjectives and adverbs are usually placed directly before the words they modify, as in "She successfully completed the course." The same people who thunder against adverbs plunked down in the middle of infinitives remain strangely silent about other split expressions: "She has successfully completed the course." (split verb phrase) "She boasted of successfully completing the course." (split prepositional phrase) "It is better to have loved and lost than never to have loved at all." (infinitive split by helping verb). We hear no objections to such sentences because in English it is perfectly natural to place adverbial modifiers before verbs, including infinitive verbs.

I do not advocate that you go about splitting infinitives promiscuously and artlessly. But there is no point in mangling a sentence just to avoid a split infinitive. Good writers occasionally employ the construction to gain emphasis, to attain the most natural and effective word order, and to avoid ambiguity. How would you gracefully rewrite these split-infinitive sentences from recent newspapers? "By a 5–4 majority, the court voted to permit states to severely restrict women's rights to choose." "It took 33 seasons for Kansas to get back to number one. It took the Jayhawks one game to almost blow it." "The Red Sox shut out the Yankees 6–0 yesterday to all but clinch the American League East division title." And this last one, written by *New York Times* word maven William Safire:

"Thus, to spell it *champing at the bit* when most people would say *chomping at the bit* is to slavishly follow outdated dictionary preferences." In my view and to my ear, you wouldn't want to revise these constructions; they are already clear and readable.

It is indeed acceptable practice to sometimes split an infinitive. If infinitive splitting makes available just the shade of meaning you desire or if avoiding the separation creates a confusing ambiguity or patent artificiality, you are entitled to happily go ahead and split!

The injunctions against terminal prepositions and cleft infinitives are among the most jumbo and stubborn of the bovines, but smaller and equally immovable critters crowd in: "*Got* is always an uncouth word." "Your work can't be done; it must be finished. That's because meat is done, not work." "A kid is a goat, not a child." "Cattle are raised; children are reared." "Human beings lie on something; inanimate objects lay there." "Never begin a sentence with a coordinating conjunction, such as *and* and *but*." "*None* always takes a singular verb." You get the idea. Dozens of syntactical sins squeak like chalk across the blackboard of so many sensibilities. Yet such proclamations exist as sheer rumor and gossip. They are never enshrined in reputable usage manuals.

A generation ago, the airwaves were filled with a little jingle that twanged, "Winston tastes good like a cigarette should." English teachers and other word watchers raised such a fuss about the use of *like* in the song that the publicity was worth millions to the Winston people. So the cigarette hucksters came back with a second campaign: "What do you want—good grammar or good taste?"

My answer to that question is that the use of *like* in the Winston commercial is both good grammar (really, good usage) *and* in good taste.

Among prescriptive grammarians the prevailing rule is that we may use *like* or *as* as a preposition joining a noun—*cleans like a white tornado, blind as a bat*—but we must not use *like* as a conjunction that introduces an adverb clause: The son-of-Winston commercial slogan *Nobody can do it like McDonald's can* is unacceptable because the sentence doesn't sound good like a conjunction should.

Even princes have been royally reprimanded for violating this admonition. Back in the nineteenth century the poet laureate Alfred, Lord Tennyson told the linguist F. J. Furnivall, "It's a modern vulgarism that I have seen grow up within the last thirty years; and when Prince Albert used it in my drawing room, I pulled him up for it, in the presence of the Queen, and told him he never ought to use it again." Tennyson's adamance about the "rule" is preserved by the panel for the *Harper Dictionary of Contemporary Usage*. These 166 distinguished language experts condemned the use of *like* as a conjunction 72–28 percent in casual speech and 88–12 percent in writing.

Cheeky as it may appear, I take issue with the lineup of linguistic luminaries, ranging from Isaac Asimov to William Zinsser. Any open-minded, open-eared observer of the living English language cannot fail to notice that tens of everyday expressions employ *like* as a subordinating conjunction. Fill in the following blanks:

- He tells it _____ it is.

- She ate _____ there was no tomorrow.

- If you knew Suzie _____ I know Suzie . . .

- They make the food here just _____ my mother used to.

And what about *Winston tastes good* _____ *a cigarette should* and *Nobody can do it* _____ *McDonald's can?* I am confident that, despite the fact that each blank kicks off an adverb clause, most native English speakers would naturally supply *like*. If I'm wrong, then I guess I don't know my *as* from a hole in the ground.

By now you must be thinking that I am a flaming permissivist who adopts as a household pet any new use that crawls out of the language wordwork. But in truth I constantly fight the good fight to maintain precise differences between the likes of *less* and *fewer* and *I, me,* and *myself.* These are useful distinctions to which the majority of educated speakers and writers continue to adhere. Words are themselves ideas pulsing with particular recognitions and energies that enlarge and quicken life. Blur shades of meaning in language and you blur shades of thinking.

For many years I served as vice president of SPELL— Society for the Preservation of English Language and Literature. Founded in 1984, SPELL is an international corps of word-watchers dedicated to the proper use and usage of the mother tongue. In pursuit of this lofty goal, SPELL has conferred Dunce Cap Awards on perpetrators of especially egregious errors in usage, spelling, and punctuation inflicted on the public's sensibilities.

As the lone judge for that contest, a contest that nobody wants to win, I once placed the Dunce Cap on the collective heads of ad writers for Dunkin' Donuts, a company that boasts of its products' freshness. Dunkin' Donuts ran a radio and television commercial explaining that "the problem with supermarket doughnuts is there's no telling how long they've been laying there."

I laid the responsibility upon all advertisers to make the

proper choices between *lie*, an intransitive verb that means "to repose," and *lay*, a transitive verb that means "to put." One lays doughnuts on a supermarket shelf, but once that action is completed, the doughnuts lie there, not lay there. As one who is all for a SPELL of good English, I dunked Dunkin' Donuts for laying a grammatical egg, however fresh that egg may have been. And I am pleased to report that so many puzzled and outraged listeners and viewers responded to the commercial with letters and telephone calls that Dunkin' Donuts recast the sales pitch and replaced *laying* with *lying*. Who knows? If this trend continues, the company may one day change its name to Dunking Doughnuts.

In addition to confusable word pairs, I do not suffer gladly sentences that are riddled with structural flaws. I cringe when I hear or read dangling and misplaced modifiers, such as "Yoko Ono will talk about her husband, John Lennon, who was killed in an interview with Barbara Walters" and "Plunging a thousand feet, we saw Yosemite Falls." Was it in an interview with Barbara Walters that John Lennon was killed? Did we plummet as we gazed at the falls? Shoddy sentences like these can only confuse, as well as amuse, listeners and readers.

What I advise is that you carefully choose your usage crusades, to avoid knee-jerk reactions and knee-bending obeisance to long-ago edicts, to present rationales that generate more light than heat, and to ask why language does what it does. For instance, many well-meaning people concerned about the state of the English language react with horror against any noun that has turned into a verb. But part of the genius of English is that words can rail-jump from one part of speech to another with no apparent change in form. "I'll fax you" is more concise than "I'll send you a fax," and "Let's wallpaper the room this morning" is punchier and more efficient than "Let's put wallpaper on the walls of the room this morning."

Folks used to get huffy and puffy about the nouns-turned-verbs *to contact* and *to process*, but who today minds? What exactly is wrong with "Tom Hanks will host *Saturday Night Live* this week"? Is "Tom Hanks will be the host of *Saturday Night Live* this week" demonstrably superior? I am convinced that the converted verbs *to parent*, *to party*, and *to total* [a car] are wonderful additions to the language. On the other hand, I do wonder if *to finalize* adds anything that *to complete* or *to finish* hasn't already supplied, and I fail to see what *to author* accomplishes that *to write* doesn't. Ultimately, what I want to avoid are blanket judgments about all noun-into-verb shifts. That's because all generalizations are bad.

Oh, yes. If, throughout this disquisition, you have been wondering about whether the zoo owner should have written *mongooses* or *mongeese*, the answer is *mongooses*. *Goose*, from the Old English *gos*, and *mongoose*, from the Hindi *magus*, are etymologically unrelated. While the plural of *goose* is *geese*, the preferred plural of *mongoose* is *mongooses*. Like most native or experienced users of the English language, the fellow got it right the first time.

SEX AND THE SINGULAR
PRONOUN

You're sitting at a table and after a long period of time elapses, someone finally brings the food. Why are they called the waiter?

I've used this quip dozens of times in my talks and asked the audience if anyone has been offended by any grammatical atrocity I have uttered. Almost no one raises their hand.

Yet some purists grow apoplectic about the use of the pronoun *they* to refer to indefinite pronouns, such as *anyone*, *each*, and *everybody*, or with singular nouns, as you've just experienced (without trauma, I reckon) twice in the previous two paragraphs. Why is this usage so ubiquitous? One reason is that we have been doing it for centuries, all the way back to Middle English. It's been more than 600 years (1387) since Geoffrey Chaucer wrote, in *The Canterbury Tales*, "And whoso fyndeth hym out of swich blame, / They wol come up . . ."

It was not until the eighteenth century that *they* in its third-person singular role was disparaged. That's when such grammarians as Robert Lowth (yes, he of the antisplit-infinitive league) and Lindley Murray decreed that indefinite pronouns are singular. The reasons for this linguistic holding were more cultural than structural. In 1746, for example, John Kirkby's *Eighty Eight Grammatical Rules* included as rule no. 21 that "the male gender was more comprehensive than the female."

Thus we confront the matter of sex and the singular pronoun. While all other pronouns avoid reference to gender, the third-person-singular pronouns in English—*he* and *she*—are gender specific. We are not fully comfortable with the male chauvinist "Each student should underline in his textbooks so that he can achieve his fullest academic potential" or the clunky "Each student should underline in his or her textbooks so that he or she can achieve his or her fullest academic potential." To the most nettlesome problem in sexist language—the generic masculine pronoun—and to the grammatical stutter engendered by dancing back and forth between the sexes, *they* has long been a graceful solution: "Each student should underline in their textbooks so that they can achieve their fullest academic potential."

They has been moving toward singular senses, in the manner of *you*, which can function both singularly and plurally. That's the way we do it—and by *we* I mean we caring and careful speakers and writers. We've been doing it for centuries, and we're doing it today:

- Everyone attended the party, and they had a rockin' time.

- If somebody wants to cut class, we can't stop them.

- The cellular customer you have called has turned off their phone.

- We are required by law to post the pharmacy's number on the medication vial in case the customer has questions about their drug.

The astronomer Galileo Galilei was branded a heretic because he insisted that the Earth was not the center of the universe but, in fact, revolved around the Sun. Despite his perilous status, Galileo urged others to conduct objective experiments so that they could see the truth for themselves.

Gentle reader, please open your ears and eyes. Listen and look for statements that contain an indefinite pronoun or a singular noun and hear and see what pronoun follows. In almost every case that pronoun will be a form of *they*. We do that because the device is historically tested. We do that because it is more graceful than "he or she." And we do that because it avoids making a minority of us the linguistic norm and a majority of us a linguistic afterthought.

AN OPEN LETTER TO
ANN LANDERS

Shortly before Ann Landers's death, a reader wrote to the columnist lamenting the parlous state of current usage. In the letter, ENGLISH MAJOR IN OHIO complained of the misuse of the apostrophe to indicate a plural, as in a store sign advertising *Banana's*, and the apostrophe catastrophe of *it's*, used as a possessive pronoun rather than a contraction, as in "A great nation respects it's heritage."

Here, verbatim, is Ann Landers's reply to her concerned reader's complaint:

DEAR ENGLISH MAJOR: You are a purist, a dying breed, and I share your pain. Unfortunately, when people see a word misused or misspelled time after time, they become accustomed to it. Thanks to my readers, I've seen *grateful* misspelled so many ways, I'm not sure what is right anymore. You ask what can be done about the mistakes we see in print. The answer is, "Very little."

I immediately responded in turn to Ann Landers's response and, although I did not send my letter to her, I share with you, gentle readers, my ungentle screed:

DEAR ANN LANDERS: Knowing that you are a widely read and respected columnist who from time to time prints letters from readers about the abuse of language, I am surprised by and disappointed in your answer to "English Major in Ohio."

I am aware that English is a living language. Like a tree, language sheds its leaves and grows new ones so that it may live on. But to recognize the reality of and the need for change does not mean that we must accept the mindless permissiveness that pervades the use of English in our society.

Correct usage is written on the sand. The operative words here are *written* and *sand*. It may be that the sand will one day blow away or erode, but at any given moment the sand exists and so does the code of standard discourse.

I was graduated from high school was once the educated idiom; nowadays *I graduated from high school* is not only acceptable, but more appropriate. Many of us speak and write, *I graduated high school*, but that construction is not yet written on the sand of standard usage. *Due to* is loudly knocking on the door of the house once occupied by *because of* and, for most standard speakers and writers what was once almost universally called a lectern (from the Latin "to read") has transmogrified into a podium (from Greek, "foot").

But the differences between *Bananas* and *Banana's* and between *its* and *it's* are not the windy suspirations of what you call a purist; these differences are aspects of basic literacy. To announce to your gazillions of readers that we should shrug our collective shoulders at widespread usage errors because people become "accustomed to" them and that "very little" can be done about such atrocities is to do a disservice to the English language and those who speak and write it.

There are those who contend, "Who cares how you say or write something, as long as people understand you?" This is like saying, "Who cares what clothing you wear, as long as it keeps you warm and covers your nakedness?" But clothing does more than provide warmth and cover, just as language does more than transfer ideas. The sensible man and woman knows when to wear a business suit and when to wear a T-shirt and shorts, when to wear a tuxedo and when to wear a flannel shirt and dungarees. Both clothing and language make statements about the wearer and the user.

And the verbal choices we make can affect meaning. Anyone who strives to speak and write standard English should know the difference between *its* and *it's* because that choice may powerfully affect (not *effect*, although many writers misuse that word) the meaning of a statement, as well as the impression the writer communicates.

In the following sentences, which dog has the upper paw? (1) A clever dog knows its master. (2) A clever dog knows it's master. The answer, of course, is the second sentence, because it means "A clever dog knows it is master." The use of the apostrophe makes a crucial difference in the meaning conveyed. Moreover, such distinctions have an effect (not *affect*) on the way others view the speaker or writer. I believe that people who call themselves *relators* sell fewer houses than Realtors—and that the store that advertises *banana's* will not sell as many bananas as the one that goes *bananas*.

Centuries ago, Confucius observed: "If language is not correct, then what is said is not what is meant; if what is said is not what is meant, then what must be done remains undone; if this remains undone, morals and art will deteriorate; if justice goes astray, the people will stand about in helpless confusion. Hence, there must be no arbitrariness in what is said. This matters above everything."

I side with Confucius against the kind of confusion in language that your dismissive and permissive statement engenders. Dear Ann: Please reconsider what you wrote to that caring and careful English major in Ohio. And please don't tell us that you, who express opinions that change lives, can no longer distinguish *grateful* from *gratefull* from *greatful*.

—ENGLISH LOVER IN SAN DIEGO

UNDER A SPELL

F orskor and sevn yeerz agoe our faadherz braut forth on dhis kontinent a nue naeshun, konseevd in liberti, and dedikated to the propozishun dhat aul men are kreeaeted eekwal.

You've just read the first sentence of Abraham Lincoln's Gettysburg Address recast in the simplified spelling system proposed by Godfrey Dewey. Dr. Dewey is not the only man of good will who has proposed a significant overhaul of our "system" of English spelling. Way back in 1200, the Augustinian monk Orm developed a phonetic spelling system, and in succeeding centuries Orm's lead was followed by such luminaries as Benjamin Franklin, Theodore Roosevelt, George Bernard Shaw, and Upton Sinclair.

In *The Devil's Dictionary*, Ambrose Bierce defines *orthography* as "the science of spelling by the eye instead of the ear. Advocated with more heat than light by the outmates of every asylum for the insane." "English spelling," declares linguist Mario Pei, "is the world's most awesome mess," while Edward

Rondthaler, the inventor of the Soundspel System, labels spelling "a sort of graphic stutter we've tolerated for generations."

Nowhere is the chasm that stretches between phonology (the way we say words) and orthography (the way we spell them) better illustrated than in this eye-popping ditty about the demonic letter combination *-ough*:

Tough Stough

The wind was rough.
The cold was grough.
She kept her hands
Inside her mough.

And even though
She loved the snough,
The weather was
A heartless fough.

It chilled her through.
Her lips turned blough.
The frigid flakes
They blough and flough.

They shook each bough,
And she saw hough
The animals froze—
Each cough and sough.

While at their trough,
Just drinking brough,

Were frozen fast
Each slough and mough.

It made her hiccough—
Worse than a sticcough.
She drank hot cocoa
For an instant piccough.

If the road to language heaven is paved with good intentions, why haven't we Americans responded to the succession of well-intentioned spelling reforms proposed by linguists, clerics, writers, statesmen, and presidents? Because, as in most matters linguistic, simplified spelling is no simple matter.

For one thing, spelling reform would plunder the richness of homophones in the English language. *Rain, rein,* and *reign* were once pronounced differently, but time has made them sound alike. *Knight* was a logical spelling in Chaucer's day, when the *k, n,* and *gh* were distinctly sounded. Today its pronunciation matches that of *night.* In Milton's time, *colonel* was spoken with all three syllables. Now it sounds the same as *kernel.* Thus, the seemingly bizarre spellings that the reformers would excise are actually an aid to differentiation in writing. Think, for example, of the chaos that would be wrought by spelling the antonyms *raise* and *raze* identically.

So-called simplified spelling turns out to be a snare and a delusion of false simplicity. Instituting such reforms would generate a "big bang" effect, blowing apart words that are currently related. Like the builders of the Tower of Babel, lexical neighbors such as *nature* and *natural* would, as *naechur* and *nachurul,* be divorced and dispersed to separate parts of the dictionary. The same fate would be visited upon conversion pairs such as *record* (noun) and *record* (verb) and *progress* (noun) and *progress* (verb), and our streamlined pattern of noun and verb endings would grow needlessly complex. *Cats* and *dogs* would be transmuted into *kats* and *daugz*, *walks* and *runs* into *waulks* and *runz*, and *Pat's* and *Ted's* into *Pat's* and *Ted'z*.

Such transformations raise the specter of losing the rich etymological history that current spelling generally preserves. We cannot deny that *seyekaalogee*, *Wendzdae*, and *troosoe* are accurate visualizations of the sounds they represent. But do we really want to banish the Greekness from *psychology* (from the Greek goddess Psyche), the Scandinavianness from *Wednesday* (from the Norse god Woden), and the romantic Frenchness from *trousseau*?

English is the most hospitable and democratic language that has ever existed. It has welcomed into its vocabulary words from tens of other languages and dialects, far and near, ancient and modern. As Carl Sandburg once observed, "The English language hasn't got where it is by being pure." As James D. Nicoll has quipped, "The problem with defending the purity of English is that English is as pure as a cribhouse whore. We don't just borrow words. On occasion, English has pursued other languages down alleyways to beat them unconscious and rifle their pockets for new vocabulary." Purifying our spelling system would obscure our long history of exuberant borrowing.

A perhaps more telling fret in the armor of simplified spelling is that even its most ardent adherents acknowledge that many words, such as *shejl* and *skejl*, are pronounced differently in the United Kingdom and the United States, necessitating divergent spellings of the same words. Moreover, when we acknowledge the existence of Irish English, Scottish English, Welsh English, Australian English, West Indian English, and all the other world Englishes, we must wonder how many variant spellings we must live with.

Compounding the problem is that pronunciation varies widely in different parts of the same country, a reality that leads us to ask this crucial question: If we are going to embrace an exact phonetic representation of pronunciation, *whose* pronunciation is to be represented? For many Londoners, the *raen* in *Spaen* falls *maenlee* on the *plaen*, but for Eliza Doolittle and many of her cockney and Australian cousins the *rine* in *Spine* falls *minelee* on the *pline*. How will reformers decide which spellings shall prevail?

In the Middle Atlantic states, whence I hail, *cot* and *caught* are sounded distinctly as *kaat* and *kaut*. In New Hampshire, to which I moved, I often heard *kaat* for both words. Not far to my south, many Bostonians say *kaut* for both words. I say *gurl*; in Brooklyn some say *goil* (as in the charmingly reversed "The *oil* bought some *earl*"), and farther south and west they say *gal* and *gurrel*. Because our present system of spelling is as much hieroglyphic as it is phonetic, speakers of English can gaze upon *rain*, *Spain*, *mainly*, *plain*, *cot*, *caught*, and *girl* and pronounce the words in their own richly diverse ways.

Even if our spelling were altered by edict, a feat that has never been accomplished in a predominantly literate country, pronunciation would continue to change. As Samuel Johnson proclaimed so long ago, "Sounds are too volatile and subtle for legal restraints; to enchain syllables, and to lash the wind, are equally undertakings of pride." No surprise, then, that the good doctor went on to point out that spelling reformers would be taking "that for a model which is changing while they apply it." The phoneticizing process of spelling reform would itself have to be reformed every fifty or hundred years.

Errors in spelling are the most conspicuous of all defects

in written English. Even with the ubiquitousness of spell-checkers, business executives complain about the unchecked and unbridled orthography their employees generate. As a business guru once advised: "A burro is an ass. A burrow is a hole in the ground. As a writer, you are expected to know the difference."

Now gaze upon one hundred words that people in business most frequently misspell. In the lineup are very probably the words that you fear and loathe. Look over the list carefully and then circle each word that you find to be spelled incorrectly. Then compare your answers with the one you find in "Answers to Games and Quizzes" (see page 287).

1. absence	19. believe
2. accessible	20. benefit
3. accommodate	21. business
4. accumulate	22. calendar
5. achieve	23. category
6. administration	24. character
7. advantageous	25. committee
8. aggressive	26. controversial
9. analyze	27. corroborate
10. apparent	28. definitely
11. appearance	29. dependent
12. appropriate	30. description
13. argument	31. develop
14. background	32. dilemma
15. bankruptcy	33. disappear
16. basically	34. disappoint
17. before	35. dissipate
18. beginning	36. effect

37. eligible
38. embarrassing
39. environment
40. exaggerate
41. exercise
42. existence
43. experience
44. finally
45. flexible
46. forgo
47. forty
48. friend
49. gauge
50. harass
51. imitate
52. immediately
53. independent
54. interest
55. judgment
56. liaison
57. license
58. mediocre
59. millennium
60. minuscule
61. necessary
62. negligence
63. negotiable
64. noticeable
65. occasion
66. occurrence
67. omission
68. parallel
69. perseverance
70. piece
71. precede
72. privilege
73. proceed
74. publicly
75. questionnaire
76. receive
77. recommend
78. relieve
79. renown
80. repetition
81. rescind
82. rhythm
83. ridiculous
84. salable
85. secretary
86. seize
87. sentence
88. separate
89. sincerely
90. skillful
91. successful
92. supersede
93. surprise
94. their
95. threshold
96. through
97. tomorrow
98. truly
99. whether
100. writing

I BEFORE *E*, EXCEPT . . . ?

At the William Cullen Bryant school, in West Philadelphia, my seventh-grade English teacher, Mrs. Huckins,
had blue hair, wore wire-rimmed glasses and a paisley smock,
and kept an avocado seed in a glass vase on the radiator. I
wish that everyone could have a Mrs. Huckins in language
arts, for she was the light-bearing mentor who wrought order
from orthographic chaos, the lawgiver who taught me the basic spelling rules: how to drop the *y* and add *ie* in words such
as *babies* and *studied,* how to double the final consonant in
words such as *stopping* and *occurrence,* and, of course, "*i* before
e, except after *c.*" Alas, though, as I gradually attained the age
of the sere and yellow leaf, I came to realize that the last
formula did not really work. Granted that an occasional exception may prove a rule, but this rule, honored as much in
the breach as in the observance, has so many exceptions that
the exceptions bury the rule.

To begin with, the most famous of all spelling jingles has
a small amendment tacked on:

I before *e*,
Except after *c*,
Unless sounded as *a*,
As in *neighbor* and *weigh*.

The last two lines suggest aberrations such as *beige, deign, eight, feign, feint, geisha, heinous, heir, inveigh, inveigle, lei, neigh, neighbor, reign, rein, reindeer, skein, sleigh, their, veil, vein, weigh,* and *weight*. That makes twenty-three exceptions to the *i* before *e* dictum already.

Another batch of mutants consists of words in which both the *e* and the *i* are sounded: *absenteeism, agreeing, albeit, atheist, being, contemporaneity, decreeing, dyeing, fleeing, freeing, guaranteeing, pedigreeing, plebeian, reimburse, reincarnate, reinfect, reinforce, reinstate, reintegrate, reinterpret, reinvent, reinvest, reissue, reiterate, seeing, simultaneity, spontaneity, teeing,* and *treeing*. This raises the subtotal of exceptions to fifty-two, one for each week of the year.

It doesn't take a genius to realize that the *i* before *e* rule doesn't work for the names of many people and places: "Eugene *O'Neill* and Dwight D. *Eisenhower* drank 35-degree-Fahrenheit *Budweiser* and *Rheingold* in *Anaheim* and *Leicester*." We could add a long scroll of names to the cluster, such as *Stein* and *Weiss*, but we'll be lenient and count all *ei* personal names as one exception and all *ei* place names as another, bumping the subtotal of rule-flouters up to fifty-four.

"Cut the orthographic obfuscation, Lederer," I can hear you thinking. "Your last two categories of *i* before *e* violations verge on the bogus."

Very well. Here are thirty-four breaches of the observance that do not involve names, separately pronounced vowels, or a long *a* sound: *caffeine, codeine, counterfeit, eiderdown, either, feisty, foreign, forfeit, heifer, heigh ho, height, heist, herein, kaleidoscope, keister, leisure, neither, nonpareil, obeisance, onomatopoeia, protein, rein, reveille, seismograph, seize, sheikh, sleight, sovereign, stein, surfeit, therein, weir, weird,* and *wherein.*

Having accumulated eighty-eight exceptions to a spelling rule that appears to have been made to be broken, let us now attack the amendment "except after *c.*" This little disclaimer works perfectly well for words such as *receive* and *ceiling,* but what about those in which *c* is followed by *ie? agencies, ancient, aristocracies, autocracies, chancier, concierge, conscience, contingencies, currencies, democracies, emergencies, exigencies, fallacies, fancied, financier, glacier, mercies, omniscient, policies, science, society, species, sufficient,* and *tendencies.*

Now have a look at three more words of this type: *deficiencies, efficiencies,* and *proficiencies.* Note that these are all double plays, each shattering the rule twice in adjacent syllables. But we shall remain flexible and count each as only a single violation, bringing the subtotal to 115.

In the same category, if we are to move upward and outward, we shall have to consult a genius, like Albert *Einstein.* Einstein would point out that his surname is another double violation, but, having already counted all personal names as a single exception, we shall not add his. We do note, however, that an Einstein might spout arcane, abstruse words such as *beidellite, corporeity, cuneiform, deice, deictic, deionize, eidolon, femineity, gaseity, greige, hermaphrodeity, heterogeneity, homogeneity, leifite, leister, leitmotif, meiosis, mythopoeic, peiramater, reify, reive, rheic, seity, sulphureity, weibullite, xanthoproteic, zein,* and *zeitgeist* (another double exception). These handy, everyday words raise our subtotal of exceptions to 143 just one away from proving that the most renowned of all spelling aphorisms is (ahem) grossly misleading.

To show how much this rule was made to be broken, I
offer a poem that I hope will leave you spellbound:

E-I, I-E—Oh?

There's a rule that's sufficeint, proficeint, efficeint.
For all speceis of spelling in no way deficeint.
While the glaceirs of ignorace icily frown,
This soveriegn rule warms, like a thick iederdown.

On words fiesty and wierd it shines from great hieghts,
Blazes out like a beacon, or skien of ieght lights.
It gives nieghborly guidance, sceintific and fair,
To this nonpariel language, to which we are hier.

Now, a few in soceity fiegn to deride
And to forfiet thier anceint and omnisceint guide,
Diegn to worship a diety foriegn and hienous,
Whose counterfiet riegn is certain to pain us.

In our work and our liesure, our agenceis, schools,
Let us all wiegh our consceince, sieze proudly our rules!
It's plebiean to lower our standards. I'll niether
Give in or give up—and I trust you won't iether!

Now that we've reached a total of 143 violations of the *i*
before *e* rule, can we uncover one more common exception
that will bring the count to a satisfying dozen dozen? For the
answer we'll have to consult the *Deity*.

FAIRLY FAMILIAR PHRASES

Here's a game to whet your appetite—or (great expecto-rations!) wet your appetite—for spelling challenges.

The phrases below may be as familiar to you as your old stamping—or is it stomping?—grounds, but when it comes to spelling them, you may be in dire straights—or is it dire straits? Like the cat that ate cheese and then breathed into the mouse-hole, I'm sure that you're waiting with baited breath—or should that be bated breath?—and chomping (or perhaps champing?) at the bit. May your answers and mine jibe—or maybe jive?—completely so that you don't miss any by a hare's breath—or hare's breadth? or hair's breath? or hair's breadth?

Homophones and sound-alikes can often reek—or is it wreck or wreak—havoc with your spelling. In each phrase that follows, choose the preferred spelling. Answers repose in "An-swers to Games and Quizzes" (page 287). May you get your just deserts—or is that desserts?

1. anchors *away/aweigh* 2. to wait with *baited/bated* breath 3. to grin and *bare/bear* it 4. sound *bite/byte* 5. *bloc/ block* voting

6. a *ceded/seeded* player 7. *champing/chomping* at the bit 8. a full *complement/compliment* of 9. to strike a responsive *chord/cord* 10. just *deserts/desserts*

11. doesn't *faze/phase* me 12. to have a *flair/flare* for 13. *foul/fowl* weather 14. *hail/hale* and *hardy/hearty* 15. a *hair's/ hare's breadth/breath*

16. a seamless *hole/whole* 17. a friend in need is a friend *in deed/indeed* 18. to declare it doesn't *jibe/jive* 19. on the *lam/ lamb* 20. to the *manner/manor born/borne*

21. *marshal/martial* law 22. to test one's *medal/meddle/ metal/mettle* 23. *might/mite* and *mane/main* 24. beyond the *pale/pail* 25. to *peak/peek/pique* one's interest

26. *pi/pie* in the sky 27. *pidgin/pigeon* English 28. *plain/ plane* geometry 29. to *pore/pour* over an article 30. *praying/ preying* mantis

31. a matter of *principal/principle* 32. *rack/wrack* one's brain 33. to give free *rain/reign/rein* 34. *raise/raze* Cain/cane 35. to pay *rapped/rapt/wrapped* attention

36. with *reckless/wreckless* abandon 37. to *reek/wreak/wreck* havoc 38. *right/rite* of passage 39. a *shoe-/shoo-*in 40. to *sic/ sick* the dog on someone

41. *sleight/slight* of hand 42. *spit and/spitting* image 43. the old *stamping/stomping* grounds 44. to *stanch/staunch* the flow 45. dire *straights/straits*

46. a *toe-/tow-*headed youth 47. to *toe/tow* the line 48. to swear like a *trooper/trouper* 49. all in *vain/vane/vein* 50. to *wet/whet* your appetite

TOOLS OF THE TRADE

Any good worker needs good tools and the knowledge of how to use them. The carpenter relies on his or her hammer and nails, saw and wood, and plumb bob and square, the dancer on her or his pointe shoes and rosin, leotard and tutu, and barre and mirrors.

Whether or not you are a professional linguist (one who studies language scientifically) or a dedicated amateur, you have probably learned that it is not so much what you know as what you know about the sources that can tell you what you need to know. I'm now going to pull out a selection of the books I have personally found to be most helpful to my labors of love in the language vineyard. We are all workers with words, all of us who try to use language accurately and gracefully. I hope that some of the tools I'm about to unpack will make your wordwork more joyful and precise.

The great lexicographer Samuel Johnson once wrote, "Dictionaries are like watches: the worst is better than none, and the best cannot be expected to go quite true." Nowadays, more than two centuries after Dr. Johnson, most watches run quite true, and so do many dictionaries. Just as everyone who wishes to muddle along in the modern world needs to wear a watch, everyone who wants to use words in an informed manner should own a reputable, serviceable, and up-to-date dictionary. The question is which one. Because modern dictionary publishing is a highly competitive business, every imaginable size and type of dictionary is available, from fat unabridged volumes to paperback pocket editions.

The most satisfactory dictionary for all-around use is the one-volume workhorse usually identified as a "desk" or "collegiate" dictionary, containing from 90,000 to 165,000 entries. Don't let the labels *Collegiate Dictionary* or *College Dictionary* scare you off. These lexicons are useful to all readers and writers, whether or not they are attending school or are college graduates. Don't be dazzled by the name "Webster" in a dictionary title; the name itself is no guarantee of authenticity because it is now in the public domain and any publisher may use it.

The desk lexicons I most often use are *Merriam-Webster's Collegiate Dictionary*, Eleventh Edition (Springfield, Massachusetts: Merriam-Webster, 2003), the *Random House Webster's College Dictionary* (New York: Random House, 2000), *Webster's New World College Dictionary*, Fourth Edition (New York: Macmillan, 1999), and *The American Heritage Dictionary of the English Language*, 4th Edition (Boston: Houghton Mifflin, 2002).

Passionate vocabularians often plunge into the unabridged dictionaries, which average 450,000 entries and offer quantities of information not available in desk versions. Among the best-known unabridged dictionaries today are *The American Heritage Dictionary of the English Language*, 4th Edition (Boston: Houghton Mifflin, 2000), *Webster's Third New International*

Dictionary, Unabridged (Springfield, Massachusetts: Merriam-Webster, 1961), and *The Random House Dictionary of the English Language,* 2nd Edition, Unabridged (New York: Random House, 1987).

An old dictionary is like a whalebone corset, a buttonhook, spats, or a wad of Confederate money—nice to have around but of little practical use. Unless you're a collector, replace old dictionaries with ones published within the past ten years, at least.

In addition to these general dictionaries are various etymological dictionaries that show in detail where words originated and how their forms and how their meanings have changed over time.

In a class by itself is the *Oxford English Dictionary* (Oxford: Oxford University Press, continuously updated), the most comprehensive dictionary of the English language in existence. It is an undertaking that attempts to record the birth and history of every printed word in the language from the time of King Alfred (about A.D. 900) to the current date of publication.

It took seventy years to complete the original twelve-volume edition and twenty-nine years to update it in an integrated 22,000 page, twenty-volume second edition that consists of nearly 60 million words. Reduced-type one- and two-volume editions (nine or four pages compacted into each sheet, respectively) are now available, complete with magnifying glass. Volunteer workers from all over the world have participated in the massive research, sending in to the editors more than 6 million slips of paper with recorded usages. What the pyramids were to ancient Egyptian civilization, the *Oxford English Dictionary* is to English language scholarship—the most impressive collective achievement of our civilization. The difference is that inside the *OED* pulses something alive, growing, and evolving.

Easier to use and for many purposes just as helpful as the *OED* is *The Barnhart Dictionary of Etymology* (Bronx, New York: The H. W. Wilson Company, 1988). In one thick volume of 1,284 pages is packed the finest American etymological scholarship that I have encountered. While the Barnhart lexicon contains about a twentieth of the number of entries enshrined in the *OED*, the thirty thousand words therein are the ones of greatest etymological fascination and the explanations more readable. The entries omit the traditional use of abbreviations, symbols, and technical terminology and interweave thousands of linguistic and historical facts to explain the life and times of English words.

Among smaller and more popularized books of etymology, the three most useful to my work have been William and Mary Morris's *Morris Dictionary of Word and Phrase Origins*, Second Edition (New York: HarperCollins, 1988), Christine Ammer's *Have a Nice Day—No Problem!: A Dictionary of Clichés* (New York: Dutton, 1992) and Robert Hendrickson's *Facts on File Encyclopedia of Word and Phrase Origins* (New York: Facts on File Publications, 1987). Within these lexicons wink out phrases and expressions that one can't always find in the *OED*.

One who is fascinated by the origins and development of words will usually want to place that evolution in the context of the history of the English language. The popular histories that have most influenced me are Lincoln Barnett's *The Treasure of Our Tongue* (New York: Alfred A. Knopf, 1964), Bill Bryson's *The Mother Tongue, English & How It Got That Way* (New York: William Morrow and Company, Inc., 1990), and Mario Pei's *The Story of the English Language* (New York: A Touchstone Book, 1968).

The starting point for anyone exploring the English grown on this side of the ocean is H. L. Mencken's monumental *The American Language*. Mencken's high-spirited encyclopedia of our idiom put American English on the linguistic map. The original work (1919–51) runs to four fat volumes and two supplements; I use the one-volume abridged edition organized by Raven I. McDavid Jr. (New York: Alfred A. Knopf, 1977).

My two favorite post-Mencken explorations of the American language are Bill Bryson's *Made in America* (New York: William Morrow and Company, Inc., 1994) and Allan Metcalf's *How We Talk: American Regional English Today* (Boston: Houghton Mifflin, 2000).

You may wish to acquire two essential dictionaries for exploring the words and phrases that travel the backroads and prowl the fringes of the American language: *Dictionary of American English* (Cambridge, Massachusetts: The Belknap Press of Harvard University Press, 1985–2002; the fifth and last volume will appear in 2008) and Robert L. Chapman's *New Dictionary of American Slang*, Third Edition (New York: HarperCollins, 1997).

Do you fret about floating your conjunctive adverbs, dangling your participles in public, and confusing *who* with *whom*, *disinterested* with *uninterested*, and *It's me* with *It is I?* With sound scholarship and straightforward common sense, a number of guidebooks catalogue and tame the demons of grammar and usage. The most thorough, exhaustive, and realistic usage elbow books that I own are *Webster's Dictionary of English Usage* (Springfield, Massachusetts: Merriam-Webster, 1989) and Bryan A. Garner's *Modern American Usage*, Second Edition (New York: Oxford University Press, 2003).

There are two sides of language—the outside and the inside. The outside is the practical employment of words that gets us through our daily lives: "Please pass the yogurt," "How much does that cost?" and the like. The inside is the recreational use of language, the part of us that enjoys having fun with the sounds, meanings, and configurations of words and letters.

"As long as we have had words, we have had wordplay," says noted logologist A. Ross Eckler. And as long as we have had wordplay, men and women have experimented with witty and whimsical verbal diversions that are both true and outré, *outré* being pig latin for *true*. For the psychically mobile verbivore who enjoys messing around with words for the fun of it, there is a shelf of recreational books that play with the sounds, meanings, and configurations of words—from puns to palindromes, anagrams to antigrams, reversagrams to lipograms, and pangrams to isograms. The modern classics in the field are Dmitri A. Borgmann's *Language on Vacation* (New York: Charles Scribner's Sons, 1965), Howard W. Bergerson's *Palindromes and Anagrams* (New York: Dover Publications, Inc., 1999), and A. Ross Eckler's *Making the Alphabet Dance* (New York: St. Martin's Press, 1999). With abashed immodesty, I'll add my *Crazy English* (New York: Pocket Books, 1998), *Get Thee to a Punnery* (Charleston, South Carolina: Wyrick & Company, 1988), and *The Word Circus* (Springfield, Massachusetts: Merriam-Webster, 1998).

For those of you who wish to expand your logophilia cyberspacially, I invite you to explore my Web site at verbivore.com. Therein you'll find that I practice the Link Lederer Art by providing links to more than sixty other English language sites that treat puns to punctuation, pronouns to pronunciation, and diction to dictionaries.

ANSWERS TO GAMES
AND QUIZZES

A GUIDE TO BRITSPEAK (PAGE 31)

1. *billion*—a million million in Britain, a thousand million in the United States; *biscuit*—cracker or cookie; *bitter*—beer; *bob*—one shilling, or a small amount of money; *braces*—suspenders; *catapult*—slingshot; *chemist*—druggist; *chips*—French fried potatoes; *crisps*—potato chips; *dinner jacket*—tuxedo; *full stop*—period; *ground floor*—first floor; *hockey*—ice hockey; *ice*—ice cream; *jelly*—gelatin dessert; *knickers*—women's underpants; *lift*—elevator; M.P.—member of parliament; *minister*—cabinet member; *plaster*—Band-Aid; *pocketbook*—pocket notebook or billfold; *public school*—private school; *pudding*—dessert; *spectacles*—eye glasses; *stone*—fourteen pounds; *stuff*—unprintable in this respectable book; *sweet*—dessert; *till*—cash register; *tin*—can; *torch*—flashlight; *vest*—undershirt; *waistcoat*—vest.

2. *aisle*—gangway; *bar*—pub; *bathroom*—loo or WC (water closet); *bobby pin*—hair grip; *clothespin*—clothes-peg; *counterclockwise*—anti-clockwise; *hardware store*—ironmonger; *intermission*—interval; *kerosene*—paraffin; *napkin*—serviette; *quilt*—eiderdown; *shrimp*—

prawn; *silverware*—cutlery; *sled*—sledge; *swimsuit*—swim costume; *telephone booth*—call-box or telephone kiosk; *thumbtack*—drawing pin or push-pin; *zero*—zed.

3. *advert*—advertisement; *banger*—sausage; *bobby*—policeman; *chucker-out*—bouncer; *don*—college teacher; *draughts*—checkers; *dressing gown*—bathrobe; *dustbin*—trash can; *fortnight*—two weeks; *hoover*—vacuum cleaner; *plimsolls*—sneakers; *porridge*—oatmeal; *pram*—baby carriage; *scone*—baking-powder biscuit; *spanner*—wrench; *starter*—appetizer; *switchback*—roller coaster; *takeaway*—take-out; *telly*—television.

4. ett, bean, bown, clark, dyutee, eyethur, eevohlushun, feah, figger, GArage, herb (with the *h* sounded), labORatory (five syllables), lezhur, leftenant, missyle, pahtriot, prihvacee (short *i*), shedule, SECretry (three syllables), sujjest, tomahto (but potayto), vihtamin (short *i*), zehbra.

5. aeroplane, aluminium, cheque, defence, fibre, grey, inflexion, enquire, gaol, jewellery, judgement, manoeuvre, marvellous, organisation, pyjamas, plough, programme, speciality, spelt, storey, tonnes, phial, whisky.

6. Japan are leading the world in exports, different to, in hospital, living in Baker Street.

7.

a.   Put some gravy on my beef.

b.   My compliments to the cook.

c.   In his hand he held a pistol.

d.   That's worth a lot of money.

e.   Bring the food to the table.

f.   How about a game of darts?

g.   Do you hear me, or are you deaf?

h.   Boil me some potatoes for lunch.

i.   I'm dead on my feet.

j.   That's one of my favorite songs.

k. You're a darned liar.

l. It's around the next corner.

m. How are the wife and the kids?

n. Please pass the bread, the butter, and the cheese.

o. If you drink too many of those bitters, you'll get drunk.

A WORDY WEEKEND (PAGE 94)

1. Unfinished business.

2. Split-second timing.

3. Truth is stranger than fiction.

4. Put it in writing.

5. Parting of the ways.

6. Keeping body and soul together.

7. Blood is thicker than water.

8. Two jumps ahead of the sheriff.

9. Right between the eyes.

10. Leave well enough alone.

11. A drop in the bucket.

12. The buck stops here.

WORDS THAT NEVER STRAY (PAGE 123)

1. run amok 2. look askance 3. take umbrage 4. bide one's time 5. inner sanctum 6. arms akimbo 7. under the auspices of 8. ulterior motive 9. taken aback 10. malice aforethought.
11. in a tizzy 12. go haywire 13. slim pickings 14. in cahoots

15. from time immemorial   16. country bumpkin   17. old geezer   18. wax wroth   19. in the throes of   20. at loggerheads.

21. in a trice   22. have one's druthers   23. good riddance   24. by dint of   25. in the offing   26. at one's behest   27. a whole nother   28. on the lam   29. whisper sweet nothings   30. take a breather.

31. hugh muckamuck   32. vantage point   33. taken unawares 34. misspent youth   35. treasure trove   36. wishful thinking   37. gainful employment   38. barefaced lie   39. wend one's way   40. wreak havoc.

41. unsung hero   42. foregone conclusion   43. scot-free   44. briny deep   45. lickety-split   46. busman's holiday   47. ride roughshod   48. breakneck speed   49. blithering idiot   50. sleight of hand.

51. put the kibosh on   52. coffee klatch   53. on bended knee 54. high dudgeon   55. in arrears   56. chock-full   57. dipsy doodle 58. Pyrrhic victory   59. as is one's wont   60. workaday world.

61. Let bygones be bygones   62. He went thataway   63. the whole shebang   64. fatted calf   65. graven image   66. artesian well 67. pinking shears   68. suborn perjury   69. moral suasion   70. scruff of the neck.

71. anchors aweigh   72. super-duper   73. nitty-gritty   74. tick-tock   75. acid reflux   76. raring to go   77. knockdown dragout   78. gibbous moon   79. days of yore   80. circadian rhythms.

81. full-fledged   82. swaddling clothes   83. self-fulfilling prophecy   84. to the nth degree   85. self-aggrandizement   86. fair to middling   87. macular degeneration   88. sleep apnea   89. neap tide 90. quote unquote.

91. beck and call   92. spick and span   93. null and void   94. vim and vigor   95. kith and kin   96. betwixt and between   97. bib and tucker   98. hem and haw   99. whys and wherefores   100. hither

and yon   101. hither and thither   102. kit and kaboodle   103. to and fro   104. aid and abet   105. alas and alack.

THE NAME IS THE GAME (PAGE 202)

1. Halle Berry   2. Beau Bridges   3. John Candy   4. Jim Carrey
5. Chevy Chase.

6. Glenn Close   7. Noel Coward   8. Russell Crowe   9. Tom Cruise   10. Billy Crystal.

11. John Derek   12. Minnie Driver   13. Farrah Fawcett   14. W. C. Fields   15. Cary Grant.

16. Gene Hackman   17. Gabby Hayes   18. Celeste Holm   19. Bob Hope   20. Rock Hudson.

21. Tab Hunter   22. Ruby Keeler   23. Rob Lowe   24. Victor Mature   25. Bette Midler.

26. Tom Mix   27. John Payne   28. Brad Pitt   29. Brooke Shields   30. Red Skelton.

31. Rip Torn   32. Tuesday Weld   33. Gene Wilder   34. Shelley Winters   35. Natalie Wood.

UNDER A SPELL (PAGE 268)

All the words in the list are spelled correctly. If you just happened to circle some of the words, compare your vision of each circled item with each spelling given. That way you'll go a long way in taming some of your personal spelling demons.

FAIRLY FAMILIAR PHRASES (PAGE 275)

If any of your answers don't jibe with those listed below, check their definitions in your dictionary.

1. *aweigh* 2. *bated* 3. *bear* 4. *bite* 5. *bloc.*

6. *seeded* 7. *champing* or *chomping* 8. *complement* 9. *chord* 10. *deserts.*

11. *faze* 12. *flair* 13. *foul* 14. *hail/hearty* 15. *hair's breadth.*

16. *whole* 17. *indeed* 18. *jibe* 19. *lam* 20. *manner born.*

21. *martial* 22. *mettle* 23. *might/main* 24. *pale* 25. *pique.*

26. *pie* 27. *pidgin* 28. *plane* 29. *pore* 30. *praying.*

31. *principle* 32. *rack* 33. *rein* 34. *raise Cain* 35. *rapt.*

36. *reckless* 37. *wreak* 38. *rite* 39. *shoo* 40. *sic.*

41. *sleight* 42. *spitting* 43. *stamping* 44. *stanch* 45. *straits.*

46. *tow* 47. *toe* 48. *trooper* 49. *vain* 50. *whet.*